GW01217413

PLANETVEIEN 12

ELISABETH TOSTRUP

PLANETVEIEN 12

THE KORSMO HOUSE
A SCANDINAVIAN ICON

Artifice
books on architecture

"Life in Planetveien", by Gunnar S Gundersen

CONTENTS

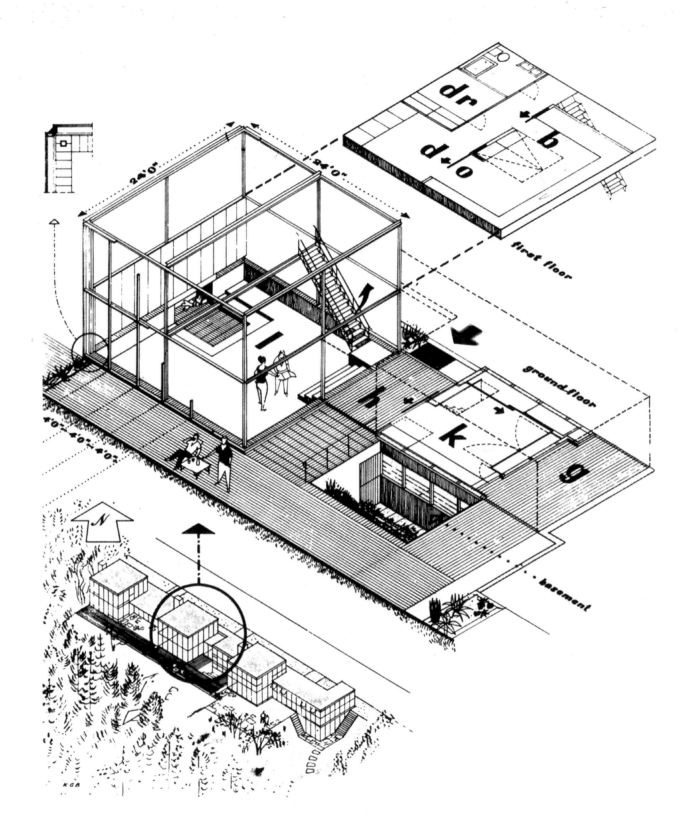

first floor

ground floor

basement

24'0"

24'0"

4'0" 4'0" 4'0"

dr

d o

b

h

k

g

N

KGB

FOREWORD

Learning to see was central to the philosophy of the architect and teacher Arne Korsmo. I was fortunate enough to be one of Korsmo's students, and also worked as a student assistant, and later a lecturer in his department at the Norwegian Institute of Technology during the 1960s. Accordingly, and in all modesty, I have taken learning to see as my starting point in my attempt to understand Arne Korsmo and Grete Prytz Kittelsen's house at Planetveien 12 and to illuminate the unique features of its architecture. The house has appeared in many publications and has been the subject of much discussion during the nearly 60 years since it was built. My aim in this book is to augment and enhance our knowledge about the house, thereby enabling a deeper understanding of its architecture and surroundings.

My study of the house and related materials has been a true journey of discovery and many people have assisted me along the way. Foremost among them was Grete Prytz Kittelsen, the owner of the house and my second cousin. A charming, quick-witted and subtle provider of information, she allowed me to visit repeatedly and even to stay overnight so that I could experience the house in different situations. We talked many times and at length about the house and its history before she passed away in the autumn of 2010. Many thanks are also due to the architect Hanne Refsdal, Arne Korsmo's widow, for many very helpful conversations and for the readiness of both her and her daughters, Anne-Lin and Marie Korsmo, to make available original drawings and photographs.

The architects Finn Kolstad and Terje Moe, both of whom were acquaintances from my time studying in Korsmo's department in Trondheim, and who later became professors at the Oslo School of Architecture and Design and the Norwegian University of Science and Technology respectively, have both been of invaluable assistance in discussing archival materials in a broader social and cultural context. I have also benefited greatly from my participation in the "Network for Norwegian architecture and design 1950–1970", led by Espen Johnsen at the University of Oslo. The activities of this network, which included seminars and field trips over a period of several years, culminated in the exhibition Brytninger. Norsk arkitektur 1945–1965 (Upheaval. Norwegian architecture 1945–1965) at the National Museum for Art, Architecture and Design in 2010–2011. The major volume *Grete Prytz Kittelsen: emalje-design*, published in 2008, has also been a very valuable source for my research. The National Museum—Architecture has been very helpful in allowing me access to its archives. In addition I would like to thank the Oslo School of Architecture and Design (AHO) for enabling me to work on this book project and use it in my teaching.

The original drawings for the house were available, but had not been updated during its actual construction. Accordingly I am very grateful to the AHO's Institute of Form, Theory and History, which in the spring of 2011 as part of its survey course "Tectonic traditions", assigned a group of students to survey and prepare new drawings of Planetveien 12. These survey drawings were prepared for publication by Ole Marius Manskow Løken and Mathilde Dahl. During this process, the new owners of the house, Mikkel Orheim and Ida Gullhav, were generous in allowing access. Their interest and energy augur well for the success of initiatives to preserve the house and its architectural qualities in collaboration with the authorities responsible for protecting our cultural heritage. I would also like to thank Pax Forlag for the original Norwegian edition of the book and for their work in guiding the editorial process. And last, but not least, I would like to thank Artifice books on architecture for publishing this English language edition.

Korsmo's axonometric drawing of no.12 Planetveien.

Oslo, March 2014, Elisabeth Tostrup

1 • AT THE FOREST'S EDGE

Many visitors have been entranced by the row of three white attached houses in Planetveien ("Planet Road") in Oslo. The houses, which were built in the mid-1950s, were designed by the architects Arne Korsmo and Christian Norberg-Schulz for themselves and their families. Particularly fascinating is Arne Korsmo's house, no. 12, in the middle of the row.

One reason for many people's interest in this house is the fact that for more than 50 years it was the home of the enamel artist Grete Prytz Kittelsen. She had been married to Korsmo and the house was their joint project. After the couple divorced in 1960, Grete Prytz Korsmo, subsequently Kittelsen, continued to live there. During the ensuing period of over 50 years, she took reverential care of the house, giving careful consideration to even the most minor alterations. She was also very generous in opening her doors to architecture students, friends and acquaintances—many of whom had an interest in art, design and architecture.

But the main reason for the widespread enthusiasm about the house is quite simply that its architecture transcends the solutions typical of its time: Korsmo's house at the forest's edge clearly deserves its reputation as a pearl of architecture. In this book we focus on the house's architectonic qualities. What are the key elements of the architecture? What principles determine the overall layout and structure? And how do choices of materials and design solutions influence the different spatial environments within the house?

Planetveien 12 has featured in many Norwegian and international publications, usually by means of photographs with accompanying brief descriptions. Frequently it is described as a "live-work home", as an example of the "Home Meccano" method, or as an "experimental house in steel and glass". In the following we examine these concepts and ideals, and their influence on the architecture of the house. Our starting point is the 1950s, which was a watershed decade for Norwegian architecture and design. The volume of reconstruction in the years immediately following the Second World War necessitated rationing of building materials. In time the most stringent of these restrictions were relaxed and Norwegians began to resume contacts abroad, not least with the United States. These contacts were to be of decisive significance for the design of the row of attached houses in Planetveien. Another important factor was the receptiveness of the Norwegian architecture and design community, in which the Korsmos were active and central participants, to impulses from outside Norway.

We will look more closely both at these impulses and at general trends in architecture at that time, but not until we have taken a "guided tour" of Planetveien 12. We will visit it early in the twenty-first century, seeing the house as it was in the final years of Grete Prytz Kittelsen's residence. During these years the house, its use and its immediate surroundings were documented in a series of new photographs. These photographs provide great insight into this architectural pearl at the forest's edge.

The row of houses on a winter day.

The three attached houses

Planetveien is a cul-de-sac on the outskirts of Oslo, right on the border of Nordmarka—the forest surrounding the city. Here the old Anker Road leads into the forest past a small lake called Bånntjern, with smaller paths leading off uphill towards Vettakollen. The cul-de-sac, which runs in a northerly direction, is rather flat at the point, 245 m above sea level, where the houses are located. The terrain slopes down from the side of the road, giving the houses panoramic views towards the west and south-west.

At first sight the three houses can be immediately distinguished from their neighbours, which comprise gabled wooden houses on generous, wooded plots along with some more recent, higher-density developments. The row of houses is modernist in appearance. The roofs are flat and the facades consist of white-painted panels. The framing of the panels by narrow borders of oiled wood emphasises the regularity of the modular design.[1] The houses consist of alternating one-storey and two-storey volumes that combine to form a long, homogeneous wall facing the road.

The module is the key element for the design of the facade. It establishes an easily discernable framework for the entrance doors, garage doors and windows, all of which are configured differently in each of the three houses. Each module is a half-storey wide, approximately 120 cm, and a full-storey high, with a subdivision suggested by a horizontal join halfway up each panel. A white wooden fascia board that runs continuously along the whole complex between ground and upper floor levels unifies the houses visually. The attached nature of the houses, and their separation from the road by only a four-metre-wide strip of level grass lawn and edging stone, gives an almost urban ambiance that contrasts with the rocky and forested surroundings.

Even though the dominance of the houses' shared structural design makes it difficult at first sight to distinguish among them, Korsmo's house has the most interesting and harmonious appearance.

LEFT White rowan berries in front of the glass wall.
RIGHT no.12 Planetveien.

2 • PLANETVEIEN 12

Seen from the road, the facade of no.12 is divided into rectangles, each a full module in size. On the upper floor each rectangle is filled by a white-painted "Eternit" fibre cement panel, while each rectangle on the ground floor is filled by a translucent "Thermolux" panel (three layers of glass sandwiching a coarsely woven glass-fibre fabric), plus one panel of clear window glass. The front wall of the main two-storey part of the house and of the single-storey hall lies one module's width further from the road than the single-storey structures on each side. Where the ground and upper floors meet, the area between the fascia board and the facade is filled by a canopy formed of a lattice of wooden strips. The strips cast shadows onto the translucent Thermolux panels below, which despite their milky density are reflective and give a feeling of depth.

The single panel of clear glass is positioned furthest to the right on the ground floor and creates a tall window in the living room. The adjoining house projects out towards the road at this point, creating a sheltered corner outside the window. This area of the neighbour's flank wall is lined by blue, vertically arranged, rectangular ceramic tiles (10 x 20 cm). Free-standing slender posts of black-laquered steel (35 x 40 mm) define the space beneath the lattice canopy in the area between the ground-floor facade and the lawn. This space is taken up at ground level by flowerbeds. For many years these were filled with tulips, but these were replaced by blue larkspur when the tulips proved irresistible to the increasing numbers of deer wandering down from the surrounding forest.

no.12 Planetveien with the entrance door open.

With the exception of the lattice canopy, Korsmo designed a neutral facade with only a few visually exciting elements. The shallow steps leading up from the road were originally covered with the same yellow ceramic Höganäs floor tiles as those used indoors. Nowadays, however, the steps are covered with more frost-resistant pale-grey granite slabs. The entrance door has Thermolux glass panels set in a white-painted metal frame. This sliding door was a 1970s replacement for the original hinged door, which was also made of Thermolux glass in a steel frame.[2] Movement inside the house can be seen as a play of shadows through the milky-white, translucent door panels.

The slender glass canopy projecting over the entrance is supported by narrow struts. These are attached on each side to steel posts that continue the pergola structure. A large mailbox and a small bench with a seat made of slats of oiled wood are permanently installed, one on each side of the top step. Fashioned with rounded corners of white-painted steel tubing, they provide an elegant gesture at this point of transition between public and private space. These architectonic devices add interest to the house's otherwise neutral appearance from the road, quietly awakening the viewer's curiosity and hinting at surprises concealed inside.

The "closed" appearance of the house when viewed from the road is a quality that Planetveien 12 shares with other world-famous modern houses, such as the house designed by the Swiss architect Le Corbusier for his mother by Lac Léman in Switzerland, 1923; Villa Tugendhat by the German architect Ludwig Mies van der Rohe in Brno, Czechoslovakia, 1930; and the Kingo Houses, 1956–1959, north of Copenhagen by the Danish architect Jørn Utzon. All these buildings present a closed face towards the road but open out towards the garden on the other side.[3] In a sense, all these buildings avoid what we might call "formal self-expression", having an outward appearance that is neutral and self-contained.

LEFT: The Thermolux panels, lattice canopy and blue tiles.
OPPOSITE: The entrance to the house.

TOP The bench outside the house entrance.
BOTTOM The entrance to the house.
RIGHT The view through the hall.

The hall

The Thermolux door seems to form a thin membrane between the road outside and the house's interior. Once inside, one stands in the midst of the house—at a junction with the kitchen to the left and the large living room to the right. In addition, the stairs to the upper floor lead off immediately to the right of the door. Yellow Höganäs tiles cover the floor and coconut matting fills the mat well just inside the door. Looking straight ahead, there is a view of the woods out through a glass door and across the wooden deck.[4] Over the whole hall there is a low pitch glass roof. Underneath the roof, horizontally mounted translucent plastic panels form the ceiling. Concealed light fittings allow the ceiling to be flooded with light even when it is dark outside. The quality of translucency that imbues this whole "in-between" zone of the house distinguishes it from the kitchen and the living room, allowing it to function as an area of convergence between exterior and interior. Another factor that emphasises the hall's status as a separate element in the building is the ceiling height, which is lower than in the kitchen.

Viewed as a cloakroom, the hall is rather sparsely furnished. In all the furnishings comprise three items: a hall stand for outdoor clothing; a plywood Dining Chair with Wood Legs by the American designer Charles Eames; and a basket for umbrellas and walking sticks. The teak veneer wall to the left is in fact a single large sliding door that conceals a wide cupboard for storing suitcases and other items. The ground floor is designed to give an immediate impression of the overall layout. Thereafter one may become acquainted with the individual parts of the building and explore its finer details.

The teak veneer kitchen

The kitchen is unconventional in every respect. The room is designed as a wide space, with worktops and cabinets lining the walls. The only window is set into a niche inside the cabinet nearest to the door that leads from the hall to the wooden deck. The window is only visible when a leaf that forms part of the wall of cabinets is folded out to form a table, which accommodates two to three place settings. All the kitchen cabinetry is made of teak veneer and teak mouldings. The cabinets cover the walls from floor to ceiling, giving a feeling of warmth.[5] The ceiling, which was originally covered with sheets of natural-coloured cork, is now covered with narrow slats of Oregon pine, with clearly defined spaces between each slat. A module-sized skylight, approximately120 x 240 cm, set into the ceiling in the centre of the room provides daylight. As in the hall, lamps concealed within the skylight can be illuminated when daylight is insufficient.

Everyday meals are served at the drop-leaf table next to the wall of cabinets adjoining the former garage, now a workshop. The table is ingeniously designed. From its minimum length of 26 cm, it can be folded out twice at each end to become a very long 260 cm. The width of the table narrows from 106 cm at the centre to 79 cm at each end. The table was made by the interior designer Tormod Alnæs, while he was studying with Korsmo at the National College of Applied Arts (SHKS) in Oslo during the 1940s. The Korsmos had already owned this table when living on Bygdøy (a peninsula on the western side of Oslo), where they had rented an apartment for several years until they were able to move into Planetveien 12 in 1955.

LEFT Towards the basement stairs.
RIGHT The kitchen with skylight and Tormod Alnæs folding table.

A living room suffused with nature

Three wide steps to the right of the hall lead down to the living room, the floor of which is 60 cm lower than that of the hall. The living room, which has a ceiling height of approximately 270 cm, forms a wide warm hollow and has uninterrupted views of the forest and sky to the south and west. A low concrete wall, its top covered with yellow Höganäs tiles, runs all the way around the room. The top of the wall is level with the floor of the hall and it forms the base for the eight thin (8 x 8 cm) steel columns that support the upper floor and the roof.

The most important items of furniture in the living room comprise 100 polyfoam-filled cushions (60 x 60 x 8 cm) that are covered with woollen fabric in a variety of colours. The cushions are stacked along the walls and can be combined in countless different configurations. Light from the east, which filters through the Thermolux glass panels that run along most of the wall facing the road, provides ever-changing effects of light and shadow. The wall adjoining number 14 (originally Norberg-Schulz's house) is fitted with shallow cupboards. These have specially hinged reversible doors that allow the surface facing into the room to be either white or black. Moveable perforated steel rods allow teak shelves to be hung at various heights in front of the cupboards. The cupboard doors also serve as display panels for pictures. Along this wall, and recessed more deeply into the neighbouring house, there is a wide fireplace. The area in front of the fireplace is two steps down from the rest of the room and is tiled with yellow fire-proof brick.

The living room seen from the hall.

The steps form a seating area around a low table made of wide planks of teak in front of the fireplace. The floor in the rest of the room has grey carpeting laid wall-to-wall over the cast concrete floor, which has a warm-water underfloor heating system.

In time, as Grete Prytz Kittelsen and her second husband Sverre ("Loe") Kittelsen—and their friends—grew older, they found the low "Japanese-style" seating uncomfortable. As a result, the couple added a few items of furniture: two lightweight Ekstrem armchairs, designed by Terje Ekstrøm, and a red Italian sofa with a fold-down back. Subsequently Prytz Kittelsen also acquired an adjustable daybed. Even in extreme old age, she was still able to take pleasure in living in the house. She spent most of the day on the ground floor, enjoying both the architecture of the house and its natural surroundings.

The ceiling consists of narrow slats of Oregon pine with 25 square overhead lights recessed at equal intervals. The pine slats create an atmosphere of warmth, while at the same time reflecting the light and colours outdoors. The ceiling appears to float in space, seemingly disconnected from the loadbearing structure, with its edges precisely defined by a narrow black-painted border. A pocket in the gap between the ceiling border and the steel columns houses projection screens and blinds, which can be pulled down around the edge of the room. Full-length curtains of finely woven golden-white wool hang in soft folds in the space between the steel columns and the glass wall. These can be drawn across the wall of windows in various positions, but most often are drawn to the side. The trees outside provide beautiful natural shade from the sun.

The first impression is of a generously proportioned room that is unconventionally furnished. The room's most characteristic feature is its quality of openness towards the rest of the ground floor and the house's natural surroundings. The wall of glass windows mediates the constant variations in the shapes and colours of the wall of vegetation outside, variations that are accentuated by the shifting colours of daylight.

Along the wall of Thermolux panels facing the road, and resting on a small platform covered with coconut matting to the right of the entrance, a staircase leads up to the upper floor. The staircase is made of aluminium and was fabricated at an aircraft factory—the aim being to achieve a lightweight construction.[6] The thick blue carpeting covering the open treads gives a feeling of luxury. The staircase is strategically well-positioned for traffic within the house, while at the same time occupying little space. It also adds an element of visual interest to the room. Since the house was built, a bookcase has been added against the wall alongside the staircase. Its teak shelves allude both to the wide steps leading down to the living room and to the table in front of the fireplace. The shelves are positioned so that the Thermolux wall behind is still clearly visible.[7] The result is a satisfactorily aesthetic and functional solution to a challenging interior-design problem.

The fireplace and reversible cupboard doors.

LEFT Looking from the living room through the hall to the kitchen.
TOP A place to rest in the living room.
BOTTOM The south-west corner of the living room.

Up the stairs to the upper floor

When ascending the stairs to the upper floor, one has on one's right a large wall painting by the artist (and friend of the Korsmos) Gunnar S Gundersen, and on one's left a glass wall partitioning off the combined bedroom/design studio. The floor-to-ceiling mirror facing the top of the staircase reflects both the house's surroundings—the trees and the sky—and the wall painting. The painting makes an intense and apposite connection between the modern architecture and the surrounding nature, between town and countryside: abstracted trees, fields of sparkling white and exquisite colour—pure lemon yellow, red, sky blue and saturated black—painted in tiny mosaic-like areas and striking larger expanses, all on a pale grey ground.

On reaching the upper floor, the immediate impression is of one large room. The walls to the south and west consist entirely of windows, while the wall painting covers the wall to the east. A cupboard that originally housed two foldaway beds partitions the upstairs landing from the combined bedroom/design studio. The cupboard also contains sliding doors to close off the room more completely from the landing. Today there are ordinary beds in the bedroom and the cupboard has been converted into a wardrobe. Meanwhile the original low-level cabinets in front of the floor-to-ceiling windows echo the low concrete wall running around the living room below.

The cabinets, which have Oregon pine doors and drawer fronts and black-lacquered tops and carcasses, contain the space and form an aesthetically pleasing framework for the desks. Some of the cabinets that were originally used as plan chests have been converted to store clothing. In the 1970s, the architect Geir Grung, a friend of Prytz Kittelsen, helped her to plan the replacement of one of the windows with a sliding glass door. This was done to make it easier to ventilate the room and the work also involved dividing up and moving some of the low chests of drawers. The sliding door leads onto a small wooden balcony above the glass roof of the hall. The upper floor windows have two layers of curtains: an outer layer of pale grey light-reflecting fabric, and an inner

layer of the same golden-white wool fabric as that used in the living room. The panoramic feeling of space created by the glass walls, the low-level cabinets, the work-table surfaces and the (former) foldaway-bed cupboard creates a striking impression—open and grand, yet intimate.

The bathroom is opposite the top of the staircase, next to the wall neighbouring the house to the north. It shares an internal wall with a combined dressing and guest room, which could be accessed directly from the bathroom through two interconnecting doors. Skylights in both rooms provide daylight and ingenious design solutions make the most of the limited space. Examples include, in the dressing room, the foldaway guest bed and fitted furniture; and, in the bathroom, the sit bath, the use of black mosaic tiles to cover the floor and the walls up to dado height, and the wall-spanning mirror above the dado. Another detail consists of the stainless steel cladding used to protect one of the house's load-bearing steel columns where it runs through the bathroom.

The fitted cupboards and wall cladding on the upstairs landing, in the dressing room, and above dado-height in the bathroom are of teak veneer. The landing also features a small niche with two cross-bars set into the teak veneer wall. This curiosity, which is reminiscent of Japanese design, came from the Korsmos' former apartment on Bygdøy. Some elements of the fitted furniture in the dressing room were also recycled, either from the apartment on Bygdøy or from examples used by Korsmo for his teaching at Oslo's National College of Applied Arts. Nowadays the bathroom ceiling is of slatted Oregon pine, while the ceilings throughout the rest of the upper floor are painted white. Apart from in the bathroom, the upper floor has wall-to-wall carpeting throughout. As in the living room, there is an underfloor water heating system.

The enamel workshop, sleeping alcove and sauna

From the kitchen, a narrow carpeted staircase leads down to the basement and the workshop. A long horizontal window spans the wall of the workshop and looks out onto a terraced sunken garden: five large steps filled with plant containers leading up to the large deck behind the house. To the left, a double door with wired-glass panels leads to the boiler room, which houses a large enamelling kiln. There is also a boiler that continues to provide hot water for the underfloor heating system. The boiler runs on either electricity or oil, whichever is currently most economical. A lightweight sliding door allows one corner of the workshop to be used as a sleeping alcove for overnight guests. At one time, Sverre Kittelsen's youngest son slept there.

As desired by Grete Prytz Kittelsen, the basement also boasts a sauna with adjoining shower and toilet. The sauna is lined with cedar wood, a particularly durable timber with an exotic fragrance. The sauna has been in more-or-less daily use ever since it was installed. When semi-heated, it is perfect for a short rest after one's morning shower, as well as for drying clothes.

OPPOSITE The enamel artist's workshop.
RIGHT The cedar-lined sauna.

3 • THE LIVE-WORK HOME IN 1955

When presenting Planetveien 12 in *Byggekunst* in 1955, one of the first ideas emphasised by the house's architect was that of the "live-work home".

Even as this work of architecture is being presented to the readers of *Byggekunst*, my wife and I have embarked on a practical test of our theories regarding the 'live-work home'. (...) We have got ourselves a house that will have to be financed directly from the proceeds of work carried out each day in the allotted square metres:

1. By my wife in the basement, where she will carry out experiments and make prototypes for Tostrup [a Norwegian gold and silversmiths].

2. By us both in the kitchen (we are hoping to persuade the health board and the fire chief to allow us, in view of our special safety measures, to expand the workplace to the garage plus the kitchen). Here there are fine opportunities for metal- and woodworking using an American machine known as a 'Shop-Smith'. (...)

3. The upper floor is a design office, which has obvious links with the model-making work. We are also looking for a smaller office in town for architectural work and for maintaining direct contact with companies and design clients.

4. The living room is intended to function as a frame around our work. We can use it to test models and other items, to make drawings on the blackboard, as an auditorium for films and slideshows, as a small exhibition gallery not only for ourselves but also for our artist friends, and—as demonstrated in one of the photographs—as a 'mini-theatre' if one raises the stairs.[8]

The most specialised room in the live-work home was in the basement. This was to be used as an experimental workshop for the gold and silversmiths Jacob Tostrup, which was headed by Grete Prytz Kittelsen's father, Jacob Tostrup Prytz. Prytz Kittelsen had trained as a goldsmith and used precious metals to make jewellery and other items. She was also responsible for the company's window displays, which changed each month.[9] She did all her enamel work at Planetveien, where the new enamelling kiln was larger than the kiln at Tostrup. As the size of Prytz Kittelsen's work was limited by the capacity of the kiln, the larger kiln opened up new possibilities. The workshop also contained a forge, a propane gas tank, an acid bath and a large proofing press for printmaking.[10]

The particular architectonic concept relating to the long horizontal window provided the workbench in front of it with daylight, as well as a pleasant view close at hand. Instead of a narrow light well, Arne Korsmo required the excavation of a larger pit that became a terraced sunken garden filled with plant containers. A passage in front of the wall of the house ran between a glass door, which let daylight into the boiler room, as well as providing the workshop with an outdoor exit, and a barred iron door leading to an outdoor storage space.

OPPOSITE TOP LEFT Arne Korsmo in the terraced garden.
OPPOSITE TOP RIGHT Grete Prytz Korsmo in her workshop.
OPPOSITE BOTTOM Basement floor plan.

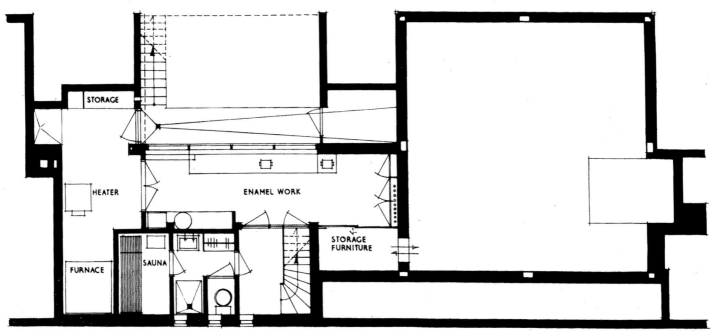

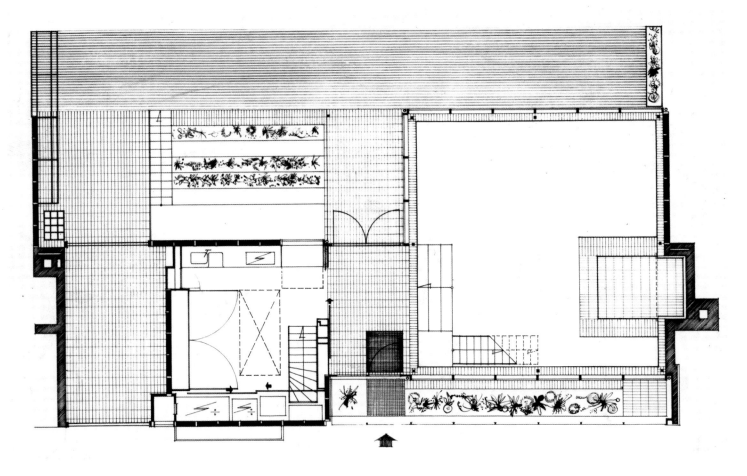

The combi-kitchen and flexible solutions

A series of photographs in the same edition of *Byggekunst* in 1955 shows how the kitchen could be used for everything from dancing to food preparation, and from metal and woodworking to laundry and ironing. This was possible because, as far as possible, the walls were made up of cupboards. This provided the maximum amount of storage space for the machines and equipment required for all these different activities, such that adequate floorspace (350 x 350 cm, less the staircase down to the basement) was available for light movable furniture and other items. In other words, this was not at all a typical kitchen for the period. In the 1950s, kitchens tended to be narrow and the layouts were designed using standardised measurements in order to minimise the number of paces a housewife needed to take between the refrigerator, kitchen sink and stove. A panel functioning as a bannister for the staircase down to the basement could be folded down to form a trapdoor. Alternatively, when entertaining, a wood panel that folded down from the wall could form an extra table or buffet counter when propped on the bannister. A further wood panel could be swung out from the wall to prevent dogs or small children from accessing the basement steps. Large teak-veneer sliding doors protected the appliances (refrigerator, freezer, washing machine and roller ironing press) from filings and sawdust when the Shop-Smith

OPPOSITE: The kitchen cabinets showing the fold-down table top.
ABOVE: Ground floor plan drawn for publication in 1955.

was in use. Similarly, the fold-down table top could be folded up over the window niche and shutters could be drawn across the kitchen sink and hob. With the shutters in place, all the walls presented flush surfaces, boxing off small items, shelves and worktops from the main room.

Other noteworthy features included a wall hatch inside the large sliding-door cupboard. Rubbish disposed of through this hatch landed in a container that city waste collectors could access through a door in the external wall. The skylight provided daylight or, when required, artificial lighting from concealed light fittings. The yellow Höganäs tiles, which were a robust flooring solution, continued uninterrupted through the hall and on to cover the low concrete wall running around the edge of the living room.

Today the room's design, which prioritised flexibility and multipurpose usage, may seem overly contrived. It was inconvenient to have to move large objects and items of equipment in order to carry out everyday tasks. For example, the trapdoor over the steps down to the basement had to be closed in order to move the ironing press out onto the floor.[11] So did the room's design features prevent it from functioning satisfactorily as a kitchen? And how did the room function in the context of life in the house as a whole? According to Prytz Kittelsen, the enjoyment more than outweighed the disadvantages.

In time, the washing machine and ironing press were relocated to the garage. This had been converted into a workspace that could be accessed from the kitchen through a narrow teak door. The garage conversion, which involved installing a large sliding glass door leading to the deck and garden, freed up space in the large sliding-door cupboard in the kitchen. This could then be used for food preparation and storage, as well as for the refrigerator and freezer. Subsequently ways have been found to fit a small dishwasher, new oven and hob into the cupboard wall opposite. Considered from the point of view of worktops and cupboard space, the kitchen can be described as compact.

The window niche—a beautiful and original design —with its fold-down table, provides an additional view. The kitchen's location in the house and its wide opening towards the hall and living room are significant. Grete Prytz Kittelsen, who very much enjoyed cooking and entertaining, was insistent that she should be able to keep in touch with goings-on in the house while she was preparing meals. The otherwise enclosed walls of the kitchen contrast with the openness of the living room and the rest of the house, whose characteristic qualities are the warmth and transparency that were such important features of Korsmo's architecture.

OPPOSITE TOP The roller ironing press standing on the basement trap door.
OPPOSITE BOTTOM Kitchen equipment located behind the sliding doors.
ABOVE The Shop-Smith in use in the kitchen.
RIGHT Dancing in the kitchen.

The bedroom and design studio

The design studio on the upper floor was depicted in *Byggekunst* with three drawing boards and plan chests positioned along the floor-to-ceiling windows. With the beds, which had wheels, folded away into their specially designed cupboards, the room otherwise consisted of a single large open space. This flowed into another room with a seating area for meeting clients. The fitted cupboards concealed a large fold-down light box. Conveniently at table height, and consisting of a lamp beneath a sheet of milk-white glass, this was essential equipment for viewing slides and preparing lectures.

The floor-to-ceiling nature of the windows in the combined bedroom/design office is demonstrated in a photograph taken before the low-level cabinets were installed. The room's office function had high priority, but it was also a fascinating place to sleep—truly among the treetops. In order not to lessen the effect of the underfloor heating, the floor-to-ceiling windows could not be opened. Two layers of curtaining were installed in an attempt to deal with the problem of heat from the sun: Swedish Iruta blinds that could be used to darken the room at night and regulate the amount of sunlight during the day, and also curtains made of creamy-grey shantung silk. "The fibres of the shantung curtain fabric are more tolerant of solar heat than any other fabric we know, making the fabric resistant to sun rot. The previously described ventilation system provides 400 m³ of air per hour to keep the air in the house fresh", wrote Korsmo.[12] The air-conditioning system is no longer in use, and both the blinds and the shantung silk curtains were replaced eventually with two layers of curtaining. The room is dimensioned to allow sufficient space to walk around the beds. In the event that a drawing board obstructed access to the beds, a sliding door on each side provided access from the upstairs landing.

The guest room, which also functioned as "the wife's dressing room", was fitted out in teak veneer. This room has a skylight of wired glass with a translucent plastic panel underneath. As in the kitchen, there are light fittings concealed within the skylight. The walls and ceiling in

OPPOSITE The bedroom/design studio.
RIGHT Looking along the upper floor landing towards G S Gundersen wall painting.
BELOW Upper floor plan

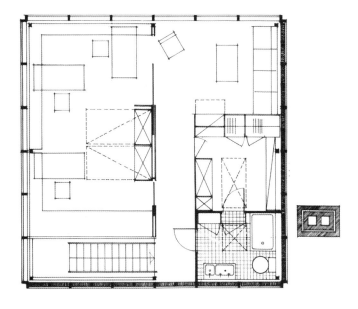

LEFT The bedroom/design studio while still unfurnished.
RIGHT Looking across the design studio to the south-west.

the bathroom were originally covered in varnished sheets of 2 mm cork for sound-proofing. The cork was later replaced on the walls by more moisture-resistant teak veneer and, on the ceiling, by slats of Oregon pine. In order to get his building loan approved, Korsmo had to indicate on his plans that it was possible to divide the upper floor into three separate bedrooms: "In this case, the windows can also be replaced with walls and windows that open (as in the other two houses)."[13] This satisfied the contemporary presumption that a new house should be suitable for a two-child family.

In spite of the emphasis on the very efficient use of floor space, there was always something of beauty to catch the eye: the way Gunnar S Gundersen's wall painting came into view at the end of the short landing, or the Japanese-style niche previously installed in the apartment on Bygdøy and here set into the wall on the landing. The upper-floor ceiling was originally covered in off-white linen—one of the colours featured in Gundersen's colour palette for the house.

As things turned out, Planetveien 12 was never used as an office as much as originally intended. Korsmo moved out in 1956 when he took up his professorship in Trondheim and the couple separated. Even so, two drawing boards were retained against the south-west-facing wall.

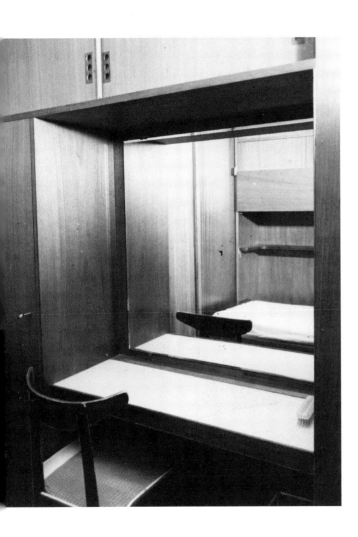

OPPOSITE Drawing by G S Gundersen: "Flexibility–planning", 1956.
LEFT The dressing room/guest room.
RIGHT The bathroom with the original cork covering on the walls and ceiling.

OPPOSITE The living room seen from the hall, with a glimpse of the garden.
RIGHT Looking south from the living room, with no. 10 in the background.

The heart of the live-work home

The living room was intended to "frame" the couple's work. The square room, which has nearly 54 m² of uninterrupted floor space and generous ceiling height, was designed to accommodate a wide range of activities and a large number of people. Reminiscent of a hollow in the landscape, the room, which has underfloor heating and which was originally carpeted with warm grey sisal, had a very special atmosphere. The room has no through traffic and the wide entrance to it was designed so that, on special occasions, the hall could function either as a stage or music podium, or together with the three broad steps down to the living room, as a seating area for an audience facing the opposite wall. Korsmo had a sense for the theatrical. He had been involved in stage and exhibition design and, in his designs for this room, brought these experiences into the heart of the home.

As mentioned in the previous chapter, various devices, including white and orange roller blinds and projection screens, are housed in a pocket in the gap between the edge of the ceiling and the external wall, just inside the free-standing steel columns. For Korsmo, the idea of "the gap" ("fugen" in Norwegian) was an important general principle. Its purpose was to separate different elements in order to avoid what Korsmo called a "train crash". The reversible cupboard doors at the back of the room could be used with the black side facing out as blackboards or with the white side facing out as display boards for pictures. As previously mentioned, shelves for exhibiting objects could be hung in front of the doors using the movable perforated steel rods that could be positioned at each cupboard module.

LEFT The south-west corner of the living room.
RIGHT The podium formed by the hall.
OPPOSITE Looking from the hall towards the living room fireplace.

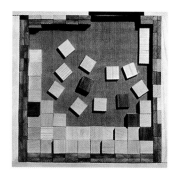

Spatial experiments in the living room

Both the aluminium staircase and the wide teak steps could be removed to create a "clean" space. The staircase could be raised up to the ceiling using a 1/4 HP motor. A grey-white canvas stretched over an Oregon pine frame could then be drawn out of the ceiling void along fixed tracks to conceal it. (The story goes that Korsmo once found himself being lifted up along with the staircase when the motor started unexpectedly.) The small platform at the bottom of the staircase could then be pushed under the hall floor, and the wide steps down to the sunken living room could either be removed or replaced with narrower steps. Korsmo's initial idea was that these three steps should also serve as the top of the coffee table in front of the fireplace. At this point Prytz Kittelsen put her foot down: she thought it would be too inconvenient to have to unscrew the steps, and

also that there would be practical problems when the steps were not in place. As a result, a separate table top was made.[14]

Furniture-wise, the 100 cushions were the means for adapting the room for its many intended purposes. Each 60 x 60 x 8 cm cushion is a soft, lightweight and flexible building block that can be moved around as required and stacked for sitting or reclining. Additional furniture consisted of lightweight wicker chairs, which could be collapsed to form "bamboo suitcases with space for a blanket", and 60 x 60 cm wicker tables. Resting on top of each wicker table was a teak veneer tray with a lip formed by a moulded edging. Each of these removable trays could also be placed on a stack of cushions to serve as an additional table. Korsmo commissioned a basket-maker to make the wicker furniture based on a photograph of an English deckchair.[15]

The architect Odd Kjeld Østbye, who had studied with Korsmo and belonged to his circle, relates that he was commissioned by Korsmo to demonstrate how the space could be used for different situations by arranging small wooden squares (each representing a cushion) on a flat model of the room, about 40 x 40 cm in size. When Korsmo suggested "Christmas party", Østbye arranged the cushions appropriately, as well as for other scenarios such as "study groups" and "Arne gives a lecture".[16] In all, nine layouts were photographed for an exhibition of the Korsmos' work in Helsinki.[17] On one occasion, Korsmo drew the house's Christmas tree in coloured chalk on one of the cupboard-door blackboards. The drawing, complete with starry sky, Northern lights, full moon and the yellow eyes of Atki, the couple's husky, glowing under the tree's branches, is still in existence. The "live-work home" that is Planetveien 12 is a radical and uncompromising demonstration of the concept of combining working and living space.

LEFT Korsmo holding the staircase.
RIGHT Odd Østbye's model to demonstrate different layouts for the room.
OPPOSITE The view from next to the fireplace.

The deck

Towards the west, a 240 cm deep deck runs across the whole width of the house, acting as a frame for the sunken garden outside the basement workshop. The deck, which enjoys sun for most of the day, is screened from the road. The view is of unspoilt terrain, with Oslo's western suburbs in the far distance. The general feeling is of spaciousness and the deck's geometrical appearance emphasises the contrast between the houses' refined architecture and the unspoilt natural surroundings. Together with the formal landscaping, the main structure of the house forms an engineered architectonic whole that stands quite separate from the surrounding nature—in the same way as the decks and interior spaces of a ship are separate from the sea but nevertheless designed to work within the surrounding elements. In his 1955 presentation, the atmosphere of refinement and civilisation is emphasised by the photograph of Korsmo—in suit and tie—carrying out the collapsible wicker chairs to sit on the deck, whose strict geometry contrasts with the untamed forest.

In these early pictures, there are no partitions between the three houses' outdoor spaces, and the deck runs continuously along the entire row. An officially registered declaration imposed a restriction on the respective owners of the three properties: "No fence or hedge at the borders between the different parts of the plot after it is subdivided shall exceed 60 cm in height."[18] When a need for greater privacy arose after a relatively short period, Korsmo designed partitions to stand on either side of his plot. These new combined screens and planters, which were custom-made using reeded glass and white-painted steel, further enhanced the spatial design.[19]

4 • PLANETVEIEN 10–14: THE TWO ARCHITECTS

Born a generation apart, the architects Christian Norberg-Schulz and Arne Korsmo were very different personalities. They met for the first time only a few years before starting work on the Planetveien project. After a childhood spent in Oslo, Norberg-Schulz travelled to Switzerland to study architecture at the ETH (Eidgenössische Technische Hochschule) in Zurich, completing his studies in 1949. Norberg-Schulz was an eager student and, when in Oslo between semesters, made a point of seeking out followers of Arne Korsmo, who at that time was teaching at Oslo's National College of Applied Arts (SHKS). Norberg-Schulz quickly became an influential figure in this milieu and was an intense contributor to their discussions about modern architecture. On returning to Oslo in 1949, he found work as Korsmo's assistant. He contributed in this capacity to projects such as the Alfredheim Girls' Home at Tåsen in Oslo. Completed in 1952, this was a low complex of buildings with shallow monopitch roofs.[20]

Christian Norberg-Schulz

Christian Norberg-Schulz had intellectual leanings that were unusual among Norwegian architects. One of his teachers had been the Swiss architectural historian Sigfried Giedion, a leading figure in CIAM (Congrès internationaux d'architecture moderne), of which Norberg-Schulz became a junior member in 1951. At an early stage of the Planetveien project, Norberg-Schulz travelled to the United States on a Fulbright scholarship with the intention of studying with the German architects Walter Gropius and Ludwig Mies van der Rohe, who were both teaching at Harvard University, in Cambridge, Massachusetts. Although Norberg-Schulz was in the United States from July 1952 until May 1953, he saw

less than he had hoped of Gropius and Mies. Instead he devoted himself to studying other subjects, including Gestalt psychology. These studies were later to prove significant for Norberg-Schulz's phenomenology-inspired theories about the "art of place"—the experience of *genius loci*.[21]

After the end of the 1950s, Norberg-Schulz's output as a practising architect was limited, although he did undertake a few small commissions independently and sometimes collaborated with other architects on large-scale construction and urban-development projects. Most of his time was devoted to the wide-ranging research that led him to become a leading architectural theorist. He maintained his pre-eminence in this field through a busy schedule of publications and guest lectures worldwide, right up until his death in 2000. Norberg-Schulz was a professor at the Oslo School of Architecture (AHO) from 1966 until 1994 and was editor of the Norwegian review of architecture *Byggekunst* (known since 2007 as *Arkitektur N*) from 1963 until 1978.[22]

OPPOSITE LEFT Christian Norberg-Schulz in no. 14 Planetveien.
OPPOSITE RIGHT no. 14 Planetveien seen from the west.

Arne Korsmo

Like Norberg-Schulz, Arne Korsmo (1900–1968) was born in Oslo (then known as Kristiania), although nearly a generation earlier. Korsmo completed his architectural studies in 1926 at the Norwegian Institute of Technology (NTH) in Trondheim. He then found work as an assistant to the architects Finn Bryn and Johan Ellefsen just at the time when modernism was starting to influence Norwegian architecture.[23]

During the spring of 1928, Korsmo spent some time working for Arnstein Arneberg and Magnus Poulsson (the architects of Oslo City Hall). The office windows overlooked Norway's first functionalist building, Skansen Restaurant, in Kontraskjæret, Oslo, designed by Lars Backer. Later in 1928, Korsmo obtained a travel grant from the Henrichsen Foundation and set off to study contemporary architecture in Europe. Initially he followed an easterly route through Berlin, Prague and Vienna, before travelling via Venice down through Italy to Sicily. On his way home in early 1929, he visited Munich, Stuttgart and Cologne, before visiting Amsterdam and Hilversum. Hilversum City Hall, then under construction to a design by the city architect Willem Marinus Dudok, proved a highlight of his trip.

On returning to Oslo in 1929, Korsmo established his own practice in partnership with Sverre Aasland, who was one year his senior. The practice quickly received numerous commissions, many of which were realised. In 1934, however, Korsmo became seriously ill with tuberculosis, and had to undergo an operation to remove much of one lung. When Korsmo returned to work in 1935, he and Aasland parted ways, each continuing with his own practice.

Korsmo's output during the 1930s is now seen to represent some of the most ground-breaking Norwegian architecture of that period. The many houses he designed, particularly in the area to the west of the new university campus at Blindern in Oslo, show a daring delight in the possibilities offered by the new language of modernist design: his asymmetrically composed buildings feature flat roofs, balconies and roof terraces

OPPOSITE Arne Korsmo teaching.
ABOVE Sketch for the entrance to the We Can exhibition.

and are characterised by smooth surfaces and large apertures. As well as his architectural work, Korsmo designed furniture, shop interiors and theatre sets. He also achieved success as an exhibition designer for his contributions to the trade and tourism exhibitions in Halden, 1936, and Moss, 1937, the Norwegian pavilion at the World Fair in Paris, 1937 and the We Can exhibition in Oslo, 1938. Given that Korsmo was also employed from 1936 as senior lecturer in Timber-based design at the National College of Applied Arts in Oslo, with special responsibility for furniture and interior design, it is no exaggeration to say that Korsmo exercised enormous influence on Norwegian design and architecture in the interwar years.

Many of the projects on Korsmo's drawing board came to an abrupt halt when the Germans occupied Norway in April 1940. During the war, Korsmo spent a year or so in Kristiansund, where as city architect he oversaw rebuilding work after the German bombing.[24] From 1944 he spent some time in Sweden, where he was given work by Paul Hedqvist, a well-known architect and urban planner in Stockholm. During this period he became close to Grete Prytz, who had fled from Norway to Sweden in 1943 due to the German occupation. Shortly before peace came in the spring of 1945 the couple married. Collaboration between the couple was extremely important for Korsmo's work in the years following the war, not least for the design of Planetveien 12.

5 • IN AMERICA

Grete and Arne Korsmo's visit to the United States during 1949–1950 was a crucial influence on their work as both designers and educators. It was also of great significance for the design of their home in Planetveien. As two of the first beneficiaries of an agreement signed by Norway and the United States in May 1949, Grete and Arne each had a Fulbright scholarship to fund a period of study at the Institute of Design in Chicago, Grete as a student and Arne as a research scholar.[25] The Institute of Design had been founded in 1938 as an experimental design school, designated the "New Bauhaus", under the leadership of the Hungarian painter and photographer Laszlo Moholy-Nagy.[26] After Moholy-Nagy's death in 1946, the Czech architect and designer Serge Chermayeff took over as director. In 1951, the Institute of Design became part of the Illinois Institute of Technology (IIT). Ludwig Mies van der Rohe was head of the architecture department and also designed buildings for the campus between 1943 and 1956.

The Korsmos rented an apartment in a skyscraper in downtown Chicago, which they used as their base. They travelled a great deal, often borrowing a small car—nicknamed "Hot Shot"—from Edgar Kaufmann Jr, an architect who was also head of the design department at the Museum of Modern Art (MoMA) in New York. Kaufmann had visited Norway the previous year and had met members of the Norwegian design milieu. It was Kaufmann who met the Korsmos when they arrived in the United States.[27]

In the United States, the whole area of architecture, design and art—and the related and inspiring fields of the psychology of perception and educational sciences—were characterised by a range and intensity that appealed strongly to the Norwegian visitors. One of countless inspirational experiences was Walter Gropius' architecture teaching at Harvard. Before Gropius left Germany at the start of the 1930s, he had reformed the Grand-Ducal Saxon School of Arts and Crafts in Weimar, Germany to become the famous school of art and design that we know today as the Bauhaus. Of equal interest were the experiments in form and colour of the Hungarian painter and designer Gyorgy Kepes and the German artist Josef Albers at the Massachusetts Institute of Technology (MIT).

The scientific studies of perception carried out by Adalbert Ames Jr at the Hanover Institute in New Hampshire also made a particularly strong impression. These studies involved systemic investigations of individuals' perceptions, when orienting themselves in space, of light, colour and distance: in short, the primary qualities of spatial experience.[28] Other important and inspiring encounters included those with the American designer James Prestini and the sculptor Alexander Calder. Prestini, who taught at the Institute of Design, was known, among other things, for his bowls and dishes of "paper-thin" wood. Calder's abstract sculptures and large-scale mobiles in steel and wood expressed time and motion—the fourth dimension of space—in pictorial terms. This was a central theme of modernism.

During a visit to Philadelphia, the couple became better acquainted with the American architect Louis Kahn, who taught at Yale. Kahn and Korsmo were the same age and had struck up a friendship after meeting in Rome during their respective study tours of Europe in 1928–1929.[29] They would meet again a number of times subsequently, including once in Japan in 1960. Some photographs

The encounter with American Modernism

survive of the latter meeting that shows Kahn and Korsmo, along with their guide Suneko, wearing kimonos.[30] Other architects with whom the Korsmos became acquainted included the Finnish-American Eero Saarinen, the Austrian-American Richard Neutra and the Spaniard Josep Luis Sert.[31]

In Chicago, the Korsmos became friendly with Edith Farnsworth. She was a leading kidney specialist at a major Chicago hospital and lived close to the Korsmos' apartment. Farnsworth's famous glass house, designed by Mies van der Rohe, had recently been completed. The house was located next to the Fox River to the west of Chicago and the Korsmos became the first overnight guests, staying there even before the furniture and curtains

Farnsworth House, Illinois, USA.

had been installed. The Korsmos and Farnsworth slept on each side of the "utility core" on temporary mattresses on the floor. During the evening a dramatic storm raged outside, and the thousands of fireflies plastered by the rain to the glass walls created an effect like a foaming, glittering starry sky. The almost unlimited contact with nature offered by the walls of glass made an enduring impression on the couple.[32]

Subsequently the Korsmos spent a weekend with Frank Lloyd Wright at Taliesin North, his combined home, farm, office and architecture school at Spring Green, Wisconsin. Kaufmann, who had been Wright's assistant at Taliesin before the war, provided the introduction to Wright. The Korsmos also visited Wright's winter base at Taliesin West in Scottsdale in the Arizona desert. The Korsmos were deeply impressed not only by Wright's architecture but also by the collective lifestyle adopted by Wright, his employees and students, whereby the professional practice and study of architecture was integrated into everyday life. This chimed with the Korsmos' ideas for a live-work home. At Taliesin, communal meals were prepared using ingredients from the private smallholding. There was also a weekly programme of events, including musical evenings and other activities. Naturally the Korsmos also visited Wright's Fallingwater, 1936, in Pennsylvania. At the time of their visit the house was still inhabited by the original client, Kaufmann's father, Edgar Kaufmann Sr.

Another highlight was the Korsmos visit to the architects and designers Charles and Ray Eames in their just-completed house in Pacific Palisades, Los Angeles. As well as a studio linked to the house, the Eames' had a large workshop known as "901" in Santa Monica. This was used for photography, full-scale model-making for furniture production, and exhibitions of their own and their employees' work.[33] The initial proposals for the house had been published in the magazine *Arts & Architecture* in December 1945 as "Case Study House # 8". Due to post-war shortages, however, the steel frames were not delivered until several years later. Meanwhile the Eames' had been frequent picnickers at the plot and

had decided to alter the design to take better account of the topography. One result was that they preserved a row of large eucalyptus trees bordering a gentle slope. The Eames' had realised that they had been in danger of making the classic architectural error: finding a beautiful plot and then ruining it with a building.[34] The new design was for two distinct volumes arranged in a linear configuration against a concrete retaining wall that runs along the edge of the plot. The two-storey front elevation, set just behind the row of eucalyptus trees, overlooks a broad meadow that runs towards the Pacific. One of Charles Eames' primary goals was to use mass-produced "off-the-shelf" materials. This concept grew out of the chair-design projects in which he had been involved since the early 1940s in collaboration with, among others, the architect Eero Saarinen.[35] The house took only a few months to build and the Eames' moved in on Christmas Eve 1949.

The Case Study House programme

The Case Study House programme was an ambitious and original project initiated by *Arts & Architecture* magazine. Since buying *California Arts & Architecture* in 1938, the publisher John Entenza had transformed the magazine into a leading advocate of modern architecture and design, with a particular focus on Southern California. In January 1945, the magazine announced the Case Study House programme and invited eight architects to design experimental houses. Five acres of land in Pacific Palisades were purchased for the first houses. These were to include a house for John Entenza, to be designed by Charles Eames and Eero Saarinen, which would have Eames' own house as its closest neighbour.

Like other countries, the United States immediately after the war experienced a surge in demand for new housing. Entenza saw this as an opportunity to promote architecture that was not only new and experimental, but that would also appeal to the general public, rather than just a privileged elite. Each house was to be open to the public for six to eight weeks following completion. Accordingly the houses would function as resources to

ABOVE Louis Kahn and Arne Korsmo in Japan.
OPPOSITE Fallingwater, Pennsylvania, USA.

inform the public about new possibilities in architectural and interior design, as well as providing advertising for the various suppliers and sponsors. The architects were also instructed to ensure that the houses could be built for a reasonable price, making them competitive with standard new-build houses.

Otherwise the programme imposed no specific demands or restrictions. The goal of the programme was simply to create a "good living environment" by experimenting with design and materials, and the programme's open approach was one factor in its success, according to the architectural historian Esther McCoy.[36] Another factor was the high quality of the participating architects. The Case Study Houses were typically designed with open-plan layouts and using non-traditional materials, such as steel, glass and plywood, as well as other lightweight cladding materials. The way that the designs for the interiors and gardens were integrated with the architecture was a contributing factor in the houses' popularity, and the first 12 houses had around 500,000 visitors. Several other Case Study Houses were realised on other plots around Los Angeles. In all, 36 were planned and, by 1963, 22 had been completed. William Wilson Wurster and Richard Neutra were two of the architects selected at the start of the project, along with Eames and Saarinen. Later younger architects joined the programme, including Raphael Soriano, Graig Elwood and Pierre Koenig.

Today the Case Study House programme is seen as a significant contributor to the history of International modernism. The rich movement that was California modernism had its roots in the United States and Europe of the 1920s and 1930s, for example, the Weissenhof housing estate in Stuttgart, 1927, the Werkbund exhibition in Vienna, 1930, and the Berliner Bauausstellung (International Architecture Exhibition), 1931.[38]

When Grete and Arne Korsmo visited Ray and Charles Eames, the first 12 Case Study Houses had been completed and were available for first-hand inspection. The two couples found that they had many ideas in common, especially those that were materialised in the Eames House. The mass-produced simplicity of the architecture,

Indigenous Mexican architecture and other sources of inspiration

together with the rich and varied effect generated by the way that the different elements were combined, and the diverse collection of objects that was assembled within "the neutral frame" resulted in an environment of exceptional warmth and charm. The architect Charles Moore wrote of Ray and Charles Eames that they "filled in the spartan framework with rich content".[39] The contrast between hi-tech modernism and folk art from distant parts of the world, represented by a collection of countless beautiful objects, fascinated the Eames' Norwegian guests. The Korsmos were also intrigued by the Eames' delight over living and working in the same surroundings. Professionally, both couples shared interests in a broad spectrum of architecture, art and design, as well as in innovative production processes and tangible results.

The Korsmos and the Eames' became good friends. In addition to admiring their inspiring, varied and extremely modern output, Grete shared with the Eames' a love of colour and parties. She later described the Eames' as having been very enthused by the comprehensive tour of Mexico that Charles had undertaken with the architect Alexander Girard. Grete also greatly admired the Eames' collection of colourful decorations from Mexico, such as figures made of folded and painted paper.

While in America the Korsmos met up with their Danish friends Jørn and Lis Utzon. The two couples purchased a second-hand car and set off along the newly opened Pan-American Highway from San Diego to Mexico City for an extended tour of Mexico and the United States. The couples had been friends since meeting in

Stockholm in 1944 and in 1949–1950 the Utzons were also in the United States on study fellowships. The ancient Zapotec capital of Monte Albán at Oaxaca in Southern Mexico and the great Mayan sacred sites of Chichén Itzá and Uxmal on the Yucatán Peninsula made a lasting impression. Huge earthworks, artificially levelled plateaux and pyramid structures with massive stone steps demonstrated how architecture had evolved out of nature as a distillation and refinement of natural forms. Korsmo often showed pictures from this trip. Although the house in Planetveien bears no obvious similarity to the Mexican structures, it does create the same feeling of steadfastness and repose in a location that similarly commands wide views of the surrounding landscape. Utzon's fascination with the artificially levelled plateaux and raised platforms, which he would later further develop in his brilliant architecture, originated in his enthusiasm for Mexico's magnificent ancient sites.[40]

Arne Korsmo's handwritten notebook, which contains drafts of many letters that he planned to send after his return home to people he had met in America, expresses his enthusiasm about the trip. Many letters include requests for photographic slides to illustrate the lectures and articles in which he would describe the inspiration and new ideas he had found in America. There are enthusiastic letters to Charles and Ray Eames; delighted comments about Alexander Girard, Eames' colleague, and the chair manufacturer Herman Miller, who presented two chairs to the Korsmos; letters to the Swiss-born artist Hugo Weber and Serge Chermayeff and many others. In a letter to Mies van der Rohe, Korsmo expresses his delight at the insights he gained into Mies' teaching methods at IIT, and says that he hopes to write an article about Mies for the Norwegian magazine *Bonytt*. Many of the letters appear in the notebook in Norwegian and were translated and typed by Grete. Korsmo wrote several articles describing his experiences in the United States. Topics he covered included design education in the United States; Charles Eames' architecture; and, in a longer article, Mies van der Rohe. The two latter articles were written in collaboration with Norberg-Schulz.[42]

Most of the letters were sent on behalf of Grete as well as Arne Korsmo. Professionally, Grete gained just as much as Arne from her time in the United States. This is evidenced by her prolific output from 1950 onwards, as well as her involvement in international activities. This involvement, among other factors, led her to become a central figure in the World Craft Council, a worldwide organisation for the applied arts that today operates under the auspices of UNESCO.[43]

OPPOSITE LEFT The Eames House, California, USA.
OPPOSITE RIGHT Case Study House #9, The Entenza House, California, USA.
BELOW Monte Albán, Oaxaca, Mexico.

6 • PRODUCTIVE WORKING CONSTELLATIONS

Arne Korsmo worked within a number of productive, and partially overlapping, "constellations", all of which influenced the design of Planetveien 12. These constellations arose in various different contexts. The first was provided by the PAGON group, which comprised some of Korsmo's former students, and by some of his international contacts. The second was his teaching activities at the National College of Applied Arts (SHKS) in Oslo. The rector of the college, where Korsmo was a head of department, was his father-in-law, Jacob Tostrup Prytz. The third was undoubtedly Korsmo's creative collaboration with Grete Prytz Kittelsen, within which we can also include a number of important design commissions for her family's gold- and silversmithing firm, J. Tostrup. In addition, Korsmo worked closely with leading figures in other areas of the arts, not least the painter Gunnar S Gundersen. The Korsmos' home was the place where these constellations would often meet.

Redesigning the apartment on Bygdøy

Before travelling to the United States, Grete and Arne Korsmo had lived for a time in a studio apartment in St Olav's Gate in central Oslo. On returning to Norway, they had the opportunity to rent a small apartment in a house in Løchenveien on Bygdøy, a peninsula on the western side of Oslo. The previous tenants had been Grete's sister Hilde and her husband Bjarne ("Bomme") Andvord Tønnesen. The apartment had one room and a kitchen on the ground floor, and a combined bedroom and studio on the upstairs. The bathroom and toilet were shared with the neighbouring apartment. The Korsmos completely redesigned the interior of the apartment, and the result was published in the architectural review *Byggekunst* in 1952. Like Planetveien 12, the redesigned apartment had a relatively large living room with a generous amount of seating that was configured along the walls. Spindly cane sofas were placed against one wall, while the wall opposite was lined with a row of lightweight dining chairs. The result was a flexible, efficient and space-saving seating solution that left a large, multi-purpose open space in the centre of the room.[44] The photographs show a nod to Japanese floor-seating culture in the form of an arrangement on a small floor rug of a large pot, a vase of flowers and a fruit dish. Tormod Alnæs' table stood next to the wall and could, as previously mentioned, be either collapsed or extended. Some features of Korsmo's experimental teaching methods were already apparent in the design of the Bygdøy apartment. In the *Byggekunst* article, he referred both to the "Home Meccano" method and to the spatial experiments he had initiated at what he referred to as the "Home and Dwelling Department" at the National College of Applied Arts.[45]

The design of the apartment in Løchenveien anticipated the house in Planetveien in that the surfaces that defined the space—the walls and ceilings—were reconfigured by means of various components that were installed inside the structural elements, like a type of lining. The living room walls were lined floor-to-ceiling by screens of white sailcloth stretched over a framework of Oregon pine. Sliding panels of white sailcloth and yellow sheet plastic were installed over the standard two- or three-pane casement windows, diffusing and softening daylight entering the room. In order to look out of the window, however, one had to slide the "lining" aside. The screens lining the walls were designed to complement

the elaborate ceiling, which was an important decorative element within the room. The ceiling consisted of large rectangular areas of white slats, louvres and sheet plastic, all bordered by frames of clear pine. Lighting fixtures were concealed in the space above the rectangles, which were arranged to leave visible an area of bare ceiling in the centre of the room. This area was covered by canvas that had been painted a deep sky blue. The fitted cupboard units, with their sliding doors and open niches, were carefully designed to serve specific functions and to generate varied spatial effects, and were integrated into the room in a way that gave them architectonic significance. The effect was a Mondrian-inspired—or, as Korsmo would have said, "Mondrianesque"—composition of rectangles in red, yellow and blue, in addition to black and white.[46]

PAGON and International Modernism

It is unclear precisely when PAGON (Progressive Architects' Group Oslo Norway) came into existence. Although Korsmo wrote, "Since 1948, a small group of architects in Oslo known as PAGON has been associated with CIAM (Congrès internationaux d'architecture moderne) and has participated at CIAM's biennial conferences", the date usually given is 1950.[47] Although Korsmo was in the United States from mid-1949 until mid-1950, it is certainly possible that the group could have formed earlier, as most of its members had studied with Korsmo at the National College of Applied Arts. Geir Grung, Sverre Fehn, Odd Kjeld Østbye and Håkon Mjelva all qualified as architects in 1949, the same year that Christian Norberg-Schulz completed his architecture studies in Zürich. In addition, the year 1948

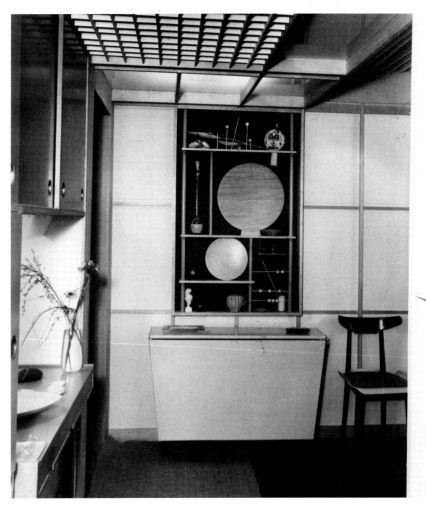

OPPOSITE The living room of the Bygdøy apartment.
TOP LEFT The wall of cupboards in the living room.
BOTTOM LEFT The other side of the wall of cupboards looking into the living room.
RIGHT The corridor leading to the living room of the Bygdøy apartment.

coincided with the visit to Norway of CIAM's general secretary, Sigfried Giedion, who gave a lecture at the Oslo Association of Architects (OAF).[48] Giedion returned to Oslo in 1950 at the invitation of PAGON. During that visit he reportedly said that he would have preferred Korsmo to have been Norway's CIAM delegate and leader of the Norwegian group, as opposed to Herman Munthe-Kaas, who had been the Norwegian delegate before the war.[49]

According to the architect Odd Kjeld Østbye, Østbye himself, along with Grung, Fehn and Mjelva, had all been active in CIAM ever since Korsmo took over as their tutor in 1945–1946. Grung and Østbye in particular had a great deal of contact with Korsmo, as did both Christian Norberg-Schulz, once he returned home from Zürich, and Jørn Utzon, when visiting from Denmark. The group often met during the evenings, initially at the college in Ullevålsveien, but subsequently at the Korsmos' apartment on Bygdøy. When the group attended CIAM's eighth congress in 1951 in Hoddesdon, a town about 30 km north of London, Østbye, Mjelva and Norberg-Schulz borrowed Korsmo's car—a white Citroën with blue hubcaps—and drove across the mountains from Oslo to Bergen. From there they took the boat to Newcastle, then drove to Hoddesdon to meet Korsmo. At the conference they were excited to be introduced to Walter Gropius, Le Corbusier and other leading architects affiliated with CIAM.[50] Korsmo forged close ties with some of his student followers and gave them extracurricular work as advisers, assistants and employees in various projects.

Odd Kjeld Østbye's account of Korsmo's first appearance as class tutor bears witness to Korsmo's charismatic teaching manner. "He came into the classroom while we were sitting at our drawing boards. We'd spent a whole year drawing bricks and timber joints, but then one day Korsmo came into the room and said: 'Right, so this is where I'm supposed to be? My job is to teach you design.' And he went on, 'As for myself, I've no idea what "design" means. Maybe you can figure out how we'll go about it? I'll come back in half an hour, and by then I'll expect you to have some suggestions.' And then he left the room."[51]

Initially, the students—at their own suggestion—embarked on designs for installing modern bathrooms and kitchens in the old wooden buildings at the Norwegian Folk Museum on Bygdøy. After a couple of weeks, however, the students abandoned this venture as hopeless and instead started to build models of various famous buildings, with the intention of learning what constituted good architecture.

Korsmo supported the students' ideas. Fehn and Østbye built a large model of the tomb of the Ancient Egyptian pharaoh Ramesses II, complete with wall-paintings and a tunnel descending into the rock face.[52] After completing their studies, several members of the group found employment at the Office of the City Architect in Oslo. At that time the city architect was Georg Greve, Geir Grung's godfather. One of his departments was responsible for designing and overseeing the construction of new municipal buildings. This work gave these young architects the opportunity to design buildings that were actually realised, while at the same time they were able to keep in close touch with new ideas and trends. Several of these architects also started to enter architecture competitions.

PAGON exerts its influence

By the time PAGON presented itself in *Byggekunst* nos. 6–7 in 1952, its membership had expanded beyond Korsmo's former students. Korsmo wanted to bring in some members "from the real world", including the architects Peter Andreas Munch (PAM) Mellbye and Erik Rolfsen. The latter had taken over as head of Oslo's urban planning department in 1947.[53] Although Mellbye and Rolfsen were sometimes rather peripheral to the group's activities, all the members stood behind the presentation in *Byggekunst*, in which all articles and projects were attributed to PAGON collectively. Despite the lack of individual attributions, it seems likely that the in-depth historical essay entitled "Concerning space in architecture" was Norberg-Schulz's work, while Korsmo's tone permeates two other articles, "Dwelling?" and "The Home Meccano method".[54] Plans for a complex

LEFT TOP AND BOTTOM PAGON's proposal for a housing development at
Arnebråtveien, Oslo.
RIGHT Redevelopment proposal for Oslo city centre, 1954–1955.

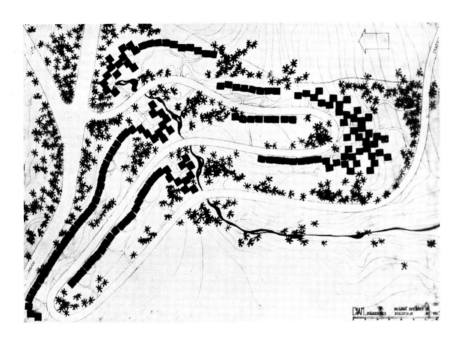

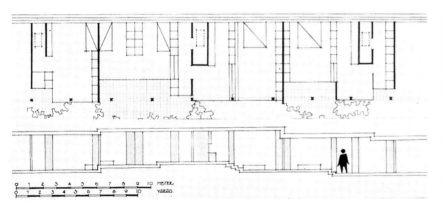

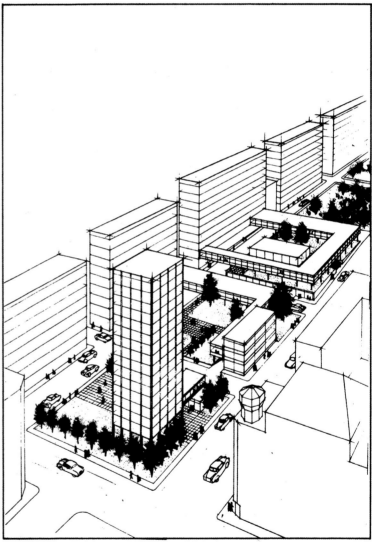

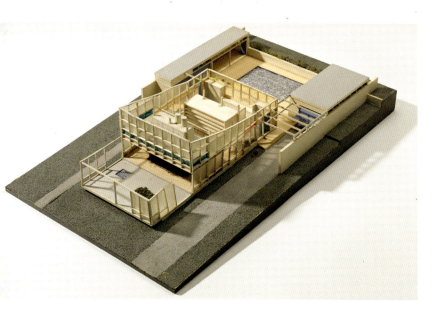

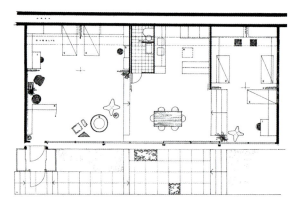

LEFT "Live-work home", model
RIGHT 80 m² apartment, National College
of Applied Arts, Oslo. Published in
Byggekunst, 1952.
OPPOSITE TOP AND BOTTOM 80 m² apartment,
National College of Applied Arts, Oslo.
Published in the college's annual report
in 1955.

of three attached houses, which are very similar to the houses in Planetveien, constituted one of the 12 projects included—without any accompanying commentary—in the group's presentation.

The articles presented in the PAGON edition of *Byggekunst*—the PAGON manifesto, an article entitled "CIAM", and others—and the manner in which they were presented, confirmed the post-war breakthrough of modernism in Norwegian architecture, which had been dominated by "New Empiricism" or "New Realism" since the second half of the 1930s.[55] The edition reflected the on-going debates within CIAM, which was preoccupied with identifying a basic philosophical approach to tackling the problems faced after the war. There was also an emphasis in these debates on the importance of growth and change, as promoted by younger members such as the Dutch architect Aldo van Eyck and the British couple Peter and Alison Smithson: "The new world requires a heightened awareness, an awareness of the four-dimensional reality of relative space."[56]

Besides the project for the row of houses, PAGON presented several larger-scale projects. Fehn and Grung's competition entry for a crematorium in Larvik, 1950, foreshadowed some significant works in Norwegian post-war modernism, including Økern Care Home (Oslo City Architect's Office/Fehn and Grung, 1955); Vettre School in Asker (Grung, 1958); the Norwegian pavilion for the Brussels World Fair (Fehn, 1956–1958); and the Museum Building at Maihaugen (Fehn and Grung, 1950–1959). These works showcased the possibilities within modernism for linking architecture to a particular place and creating characterful buildings with clean-cut designs, powerful structures and flexible spaces.

Arne Korsmo and his colleagues from PAGON worked on several urban development projects that envisaged major changes to existing urban layouts. These included an entry to a competition for an urban development plan for Vestre Vika (Korsmo and Utzon, 1947); a project for a competition concerning the use of the Akershus area (Korsmo and Norberg-Schulz, 1953); and an urban development plan for Oslo city centre from Egertorget to Jernbanetorget (Korsmo with Norberg-Schulz, Broome and Østbye, 1954–1955). The comprehensive redevelopments envisaged in these

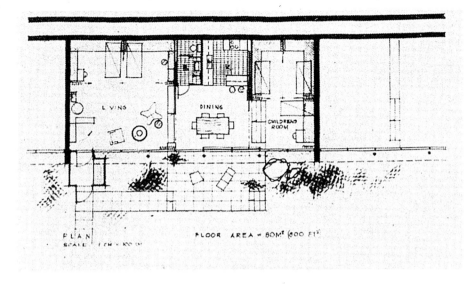

PLAN
SCALE 1 CM = 100 CM

FLOOR AREA = 80M² (800 FT²)

FRONT ELEVATION (SOUTH)

projects furthered the ideas contained in Le Corbusier's visions for urban planning from the 1920s and 1930s.

A few years later, in 1956, Fehn, Grung, Mjelva, Norberg-Schulz and Østbye, now calling themselves "Group 5", presented a number of projects in *A5— meningsblad for unge arkitekter* (a journal edited by architecture students in the Nordic countries). In the same edition of *A5*, Korsmo published what he called his "random thoughts" about theories of spatial design. As well as referring to the Belgian painter and architect Henry van de Velde, the Scottish biologist and urban-planning theorist Patrick Geddes, Le Corbusier, Gropius and Adalbert Ames Jr, Korsmo also discussed his own architectural designs in the years since 1926.[57] In the same journal, Gunnar S Gundersen described how the architect, the home-dweller and the artist collaborated

in the design of Planetveien 12, with particular emphasis on the roles of colour and materials as architectonic elements.[58]

PAGON disbanded after only a few years, and both Korsmo and Norberg-Schulz left Oslo in 1956: Korsmo to move to Trondheim, and Norberg-Schulz to move to Rome. The former members of the group stayed in touch, however, both as friends and professionally, in the latter context sometimes working together as lecturers and examiners. During the 1960s, however, Korsmo tended to refer less and less to PAGON, preferring to focus more on his international collaborations, not least those resulting from his involvement in CIAM.

Korsmo's experimental teaching methods

Korsmo's designs for the Løchenveien apartment clearly demonstrate that he had already developed his ideas about the "live-work home" and the "Home Meccano" method prior to starting work on the Planetveien project. Having been employed since 1936 at the National College of Applied Arts, in 1948 Korsmo was appointed head of the college's Department of Timber-based Design.[59] In 1945, the college had established a new 18-month course in architecture. Designed to follow on from the existing course in building design, the new National Course in Architecture (SAK) was intended to cater for aspiring architects whose studies had been disrupted by the war. Before the war, a number of graduates of the college's three-year course in building design had travelled abroad to complete their architectural training. The war had made such travel impossible, however, and the Faculty of Architecture at the Norwegian Institute of Technology in Trondheim did not have sufficient capacity to accept the necessary numbers of students. The establishment of the new course meant that, for the first time, architects could complete their professional training in Oslo. The teaching in the Department of Timber-based Design—also known as the "Wood Class"—however, tended to focus on carpentry skills, in particular furniture-making. Korsmo wrote that, "The furnishing and interior design of a dwelling and

ABOVE Foldaway bed in the 80 m² apartment, National College of Applied Arts, Oslo.
OPPOSITE TOP Living room of the 80 m² apartment, National College of Applied Arts, Oslo.
OPPOSITE BOTTOM Kitchen of the 48 m² apartment, National College of Applied Arts, Oslo.

home are included as a natural part of this teaching programme." At first Korsmo concentrated on expanding the curriculum to cover interior design more generally, as well as furniture. Subsequently, however, he steered the course more in the direction of architecture, arguing that, "the aspiring interior designer [must] also receive basic training in building construction."[60] In accordance with this philosophy, he described his course at the college as covering "furniture and spatial design".[61]

Korsmo's views were endorsed by the rector of the college, Jacob Tostrup Prytz, who was also Korsmo's father-in-law. In the college's annual report for 1952–54, Tostrup Prytz wrote that "the key factors for human development are our homes, the houses we live in and their interior design and equipment". Collaboration between the different disciplines—"primarily between furniture and interior design"—was, according to Tostrup Prytz, important "when considering developing our whole living environment through collaboration between all parties [...] and has even greater significance as a positive force for the design of our houses, home interiors, architecture and the applied arts".[62] The same annual report contains a thorough presentation of two projects undertaken by students and diploma candidates. These projects, which were both led by Korsmo, took as their starting point two apartments: one of 80 m², and one, to be used for "practical spatial studies", of 48 m². The projects were based on a proposal for an urban development plan for Arnebråtveien in the Vestre Aker district of Oslo. The plan, drawn up by the PAGON group, proposed several chains of attached housing units snaking up the hillside, all based on a 60 cm module. One of the 80 m² units was selected for construction as a full-scale "shell" in one of the classrooms at the college.

The new methods of teaching introduced by Korsmo were inspired by Walter Gropius' teaching at the Harvard Graduate School of Architecture and by the educational views of the British art critic Herbert Read. Korsmo's objectives for the projects were two-fold. On the one hand, he focused on the need, in a time of post-war austerity, to find inventive solutions when designing

layouts and ways of using furniture. Accordingly he attached importance to practical exercises involving detailed analyses of the needs of individuals and families. Fundamental to all these exercises was an assessment of the potential for using modules and standardisation. On the other hand, Korsmo intended the projects to develop "a freer view of possibilities, to release creative impulses and pleasure". This objective necessitated unorthodox methods and extended experiments to explore the perception and experience of space.[63]

The exploration of spatial perception and experience was fundamental to the three-week international "Summer Course", which took place in Oslo in June 1952. All the Nordic colleges of applied arts were represented among the 120 participants. The tutors were five professors from the Institute of Design in Chicago, which at that time was headed by the painter Hugo Weber and the architect Konrad Wachsmann. It was mainly due to the efforts of Grete Prytz Korsmo that the professors were prepared to make the transatlantic journey to teach in Oslo. Grete also participated in the course and can be seen in several photographs. The students used the 80 m² shell apartment as their studio. Norberg-Schulz wrote:

The essential objective of the summer course was to introduce to our teaching the sense of movement and space that is innate to all humans and that springs out of the freedom that is invested in all nature. To say that freedom is rhythmical quite simply means that it has order and structure while still retaining its immediate and living impulse.[64]

Music, rhythm and movement featured prominently in the programme for the summer course. In 2008, Grete still had vivid memories of Åke Stavenow, rector of Stockholm's College of the Arts (Konstfackskolan), dancing in front of the wall of blackboards.[65]

Unconventional experimental apartments

In the autumn of 1952, Korsmo set his third-year students the task of designing and installing an interior for an 80 m² unit in PAGON's proposed development in Arnebråtveien. The hypothetical inhabitants of the unit were a father, mother and four children. Using Korsmo's Home Meccano method, the students were "to attempt to fit as much as possible into the 'wall' by using cupboard units; to maximise the amount of usable floorspace by using lightweight furniture; and to leave as much free space as possible in front of the south-facing wall in order to harmonise [the layout] with the natural surroundings."[66] The amount of cupboard space required by the family members was calculated in detail with the assistance of piles of shirts, nightclothes, mittens, scarves, hats, shoes, boots and slippers, as well as cooking utensils and so on. Each item was measured and listed on a chart.[67] Two students developed—and sought to patent—a "Meccano joint" for connecting the cupboard elements.

During the spring of 1953, the shell of a 48 m² apartment, 6 x 8 m, was constructed as an "experimental practical exercise", using a load-bearing steel frame. The roof consisted of Siporex aerated concrete slabs and the walls of wood frames in 1 m modules. The apartment was designed to accommodate the caretaker, his wife and their two children: a 17-year-old son and a 15-year-old daughter. The assignment description read: "The goal was to test the effect of the 1 m module in relation [to] the external wall, partition walls and the family's belongings."[68] The completed model apartments were opened to the general public to an enthusiastic reception, at least according to Norberg-Schulz.[69] The art historian Astrid Skjerven, however, describes the reaction of the press as more reserved.[70]

According to the architect Terje Moe, who worked with Korsmo in Trondheim, the model for Korsmo's first "live-work home" was made at the National College of Applied Arts at around the same time in 1952–1953. The model is of a house with a shallow monopitch roof modular external wall and an open layout. Photographs of the model appeared both in Norberg-Schulz's book and in A5.[71]

Open-plan layouts and flexible furnishing

All these teaching-related spatial studies stressed the importance of open-plan layouts to maximise the amount of open floor space, and envisage open-plan kitchens and an external wall consisting entirely of glass modules. The limited available floor space inspired some highly inventive solutions and experimental approaches. As well as being furnished with easily moveable furniture, with tables and chairs that were partly collapsible, the rooms were also fitted out to be multipurpose. Flexibility was achieved by installing beds that folded down from wall cupboards and could be screened with drapes, while space-saving, concertina-style folding walls would allow the space to be configured differently during the day and night. The students also experimented with optical effects. For example, they created spatial accents by painting specific areas of the walls in primary colours and experimented with the placement of mirrors.

When studied closely, the drawings published in *Byggekunst* of the 80 m² apartment are rather imprecise regarding the size of the apartment and its furnishings, which has the effect of influencing the viewer's spatial perception (see page 74). The plan in *Byggekunst* indicates a scale of 1:100. Based on this scale, the floor area would be 18.5 x 8.4 m, i.e., 155 m², nearly double the apartment's stated size of 80 m². The beds on the plan would be 210 cm long, while the depth of the kitchen worktop would be 80 cm.[72] The ceiling heights, according to the section shown, would be approximately 275 cm in the central area of the apartment, which is a couple of steps above the side rooms, while the front door would be 240 cm in height. If the drawing were reduced proportionally so that the floor area became 80 m², i.e., with external dimensions of 13.4 x 6 m, this would make the beds 150 cm long (suitable only for young children) and the kitchen worktop slightly less than 60 cm in depth (as was standard in the 1950s). In *Byggekunst* this vagueness manifests itself as a visual sleight of hand, a rhetorical device that allows the rooms, and particularly the floor space, to appear larger than would actually be the case.

In the drawings published in the college's annual report three years later, the sizes of the beds are corrected, so they now appear larger in comparison to the size of the rooms (see page 75). Although these latter drawings are indistinct and to a small scale, the room depth is shown as 6 m (here three bed-lengths) instead of 8.4 m. The module for the pillars along the facade, outside the external wall, would then be 360 cm and in the glass wall 180 cm, both multiples of 60 cm. Accordingly this drawing is more plausible. It is remarkable that the drawing published in *Byggekunst* could contain such an elementary error.

Loyal assistants

The annual report produced by the National College of Applied Arts (SHKS) shows that Christian Norberg-Schulz was employed there from 1952 as a part-time lecturer in design. He delivered many lectures, while also working as an assistant at Korsmo's architecture practice.

In addition to the young architects who became members of PAGON, Korsmo met several of his other collaborators at the college. The interior designer Birger Dahl was a senior lecturer, while the interior designer Tormod Alnæs was working as an assistant in the Department of Timber-based Design. Both would collaborate with Korsmo for many years. Two students, Ragnar Myre and Bernard ("Bim") Witte, also worked as Korsmo's assistants and signed several of the working drawings for Planetveien 12. Ragnar Myre had originally been an aeronautical engineer, while Witte, who was Dutch, had originally been a potter. Moe described Witte as able to draw very rapidly with a line that looked far more precise than it really was. According to Moe, Witte's comment on his lack of precision was that "Arne will come and destroy it anyway." In contrast, Myre's drawings could appear imprecise, but were in fact completely accurate.[73] Witte moved to Trondheim when Korsmo was appointed professor there, and was to become an important member of the teaching staff in Korsmo's department. He was given responsibility for some of the practical workshop courses for first-year students and had

LEFT: Arne Korsmo and Gunnar S Gundersen at Planetveien.

ABOVE: "Mondrianesque" place settings created by Gunnar S Gundersen, and Grete and Arne Korsmo, 1957.

a reputation as a very fine model builder. According to Hanne Refsdal, "He could see straight through the clutter and identify the basic structure."[74]

Clearly, Korsmo's teaching work was highly important to his professional practice as an architect during the first decade after the war. As well as providing opportunities for experimentation through student projects, it also facilitated his work on extracurricular projects, for which he recruited students as assistants. In addition, his position at the college gave him access to a wider network of international contacts than he would have had as an architect solely engaged in private practice at that time

Gunnar S Gundersen

Gunnar S Gundersen held a unique position amongst Arne and Grete Korsmos' many collaborators. He and Arne had known each other since 1943, when Gunnar S (as he was generally known) had taken up a place at the National College of Applied Arts to study painting.

Gundersen was unusually gifted—both artistically and intellectually—and belonged to the small circle of painters who brought modern abstract painting to Norway. Before leaving his childhood home in Høyanger to study in Oslo, Gundersen had undertaken an intense period of self-directed study in Gestalt psychology and the psychology of perception, as well as in visual composition. He was a gifted linguist and became familiar with the work of leading international artists and art theorists through his voracious reading in German, English and French, including all the writings from the Bauhaus. He was very interested in "De Stijl", in particular the analytical approach of the painter Piet Mondrian and his depictions of shifting forms and colours within pictorial space.

Gundersen was involved in the design of Planetveien 12 from an early stage. His role was to determine the palette of colours to be used in the interior—for everything from minor structural elements to the 100 cushions in the living room. While the house was still under construction,

he was commissioned to create a wall-painting for the wall next to the staircase:

> With regard to my work at Grete and Arne Korsmo's house on Vettakollen just outside Oslo, right from the start everything went as well as one could possibly have hoped. As soon as I saw the slender steel frame up in the woods that marked the beginnings of the house, I started work on the possibilities that might be achievable. And so I became part of the poetic process that was to bring into existence [a building that could be used as] a dwelling and a workplace, as well as for other purposes. [...]
>
> The wall on the first floor next to the staircase was perhaps the most exciting part of the assignment. You can see part of this wall from downstairs, while from the studio upstairs it is visible through a wall of glass. Facing you through the forest, there are panoramic views—if you want to see them—of the surrounding nature, with tall pine trees and spruces and even glimpses right down to the fjord. In certain lights you may see a reflection, sometimes even a double reflection, of the wall-painting out among the trees—a phenomenon that in a quite fantastic way enhances the dynamic relativity of the space. [75]

The Korsmos and Gunnar S Gundersen collaborated on several projects during the 1950s, not least on designs for exhibitions such as the Trienniale design shows in Milan. They also collaborated on the creation of window displays for the gold- and silversmithing firm J Tostrup. Arne Korsmo's collaborations with Gunnar S also included a project—inspired by the death of Korsmo's father in 1953—to design a crematorium. Korsmo envisaged the building as standing on a gently sloping plot next to what is now Bogstad Camping in Oslo. [76] The crematorium was designed as a transparent volume of coloured glass, with glass paintings by Gunnar S encased in the double-glass walls, where "the patterns of the human mind will live on in the glass surfaces. The sunlight will illuminate the glass, and

ABOVE Life in Planetveien 12 by Gunnar S Gundersen.
OPPOSITE Proposal for a crematorium, 1953.

the deceased person will be present in it".[77] Korsmo also envisaged the building as follows: "The glass block will be reflected in the water. The painting's vertical composition will work together with the urn garden and the coloured horizontal planes."[78] The project was a study in transparent materiality, and reflected life's unpredictability and fleeting nature—two qualities that are important for the design for Planetveien 12.

Jørn and Lis Utzon

The friendship between Jørn Utzon and Arne Korsmo was of enormous benefit to both men, both personally and professionally. They had first become friends in 1944, while both were working in "exile"—Utzon from Denmark and Korsmo from Norway—for the architect Paul Hedqvist in Stockholm. As Korsmo said:

> In Jørn Utzon's bedsit in Gamla Sta'n—where, as he said himself, he was living—as a newly-wed—between thieves and robbers, I encountered a new approach to existence—one that was youthful, freer and unconventional. It took a while before—on one of our summer outings, this time to Sandhamn in the Stockholm archipelago—we really began to understand each other. Everything we found on the beach at low tide—pebbles, shards of glass and black, glistening charcoal—was assembled to make our first poem to express our shared delight in spatial experience. And once we discovered that we were speaking the same language about architecture and other experiences—it was easy to see that the result would be that we would collaborate.[79]

Korsmo and Utzon enjoyed lying on the ground, observing the choreography of the branches and twigs dancing above them and speculating about the design, structure and inherently fluctuating nature of the foliage.[80] Utzon would subsequently become famous for major works that included the Sydney Opera House. Utzon's design for the Opera House was the winning competition entry in 1957, although the building, which is now considered a masterpiece of twentieth century architecture, was not completed until 1973.

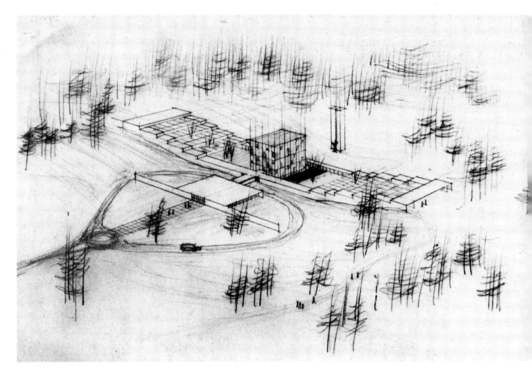

Jørn Utzon was 18 years younger than Korsmo. Although the two men had very different personalities, they were both extremely intuitive and could trigger each other's imaginations with their architectural conjectures and reflections. Of the two, Korsmo was the more inclined to speculations of a philosophical nature. Although his approach was less academically stringent than that, for example, of Norberg-Schulz, Korsmo was extremely well read and had a great interest in several scientific fields. These included mathematics and botany, as well as the psychology of perception and Gestalt psychology. Utzon was more down-to-earth and had a steadiness to him that was more in keeping with the approach of an inventive craftsman or builder. The British architect Richard Weston has emphasised the significance for Utzon of his friendship with Korsmo. According to Weston, even though the example of the Finnish architect Alvar Aalto was important for Utzon, the Danish architect undoubtedly learned just as much from Korsmo, whose pedagogical talents, inspiring style

and diverse architectural practice made him an ideal role model.[81] In 2006, Utzon wrote to Terje Moe that "Korsmo's train of thought was like the fluttering flight of a brimstone butterfly over a meadow".[82]

Utzon and Korsmo collaborated on a number of projects. These included competition entries for Oslo Central Railway Station and an area development plan for the Vestre Vika district in Oslo in 1947; a competition entry for the Gothenburg School of Business in 1948; and competition entries for a civic hall in Falköping, Sweden, and a residential area at Skøyen-Oppsal in Oslo, both in 1949. The competition entries for Oslo Central Railway Station and Vestre Vika were both submitted late, and for that reason were excluded from consideration. Utzon and Korsmo also collaborated on designing the "Grete" chair. Made of laminated wood with a canvas cover, the chair won second prize in the MoMA competition in 1948. Another collaboration involved designing a set of glass tumblers, which won second prize in a Nordic competition run by Riimäki Lasi OY, in Finland in 1949. This cross-border professional collaboration had evolved from a deep friendship. Lis and Jørn Utzon visited the Korsmos in Oslo on several occasions, and were also invited to "Jogrimen", which was Grete's family's mountain cabin at Øyerfjellet in Gudbrandsdalen.[83]

The multimedia artist Alexey Zaitzow

The former Russian army officer Alexey Zaitzow hailed from an aristocratic family and had fled from Russia to Norway during the Russian Revolution. After meeting Korsmo in 1933, he became a close friend and collaborator. Zaitzow, who had studied engineering in St Petersburg, designed extremely innovative sets and costumes for Norwegian theatre and film productions. He had also studied at the National Academy of Fine Arts in Oslo. Tutors at the academy had included Axel Revold, whose paintings were in the tradition of Cézanne and Matisse, and Zaitzow had also experimented with Cubism. From the mid-1920s, it became acceptable to undertake more modernistic and experimental work at the academy.

TOP The "Grete" chair, competition entry with J Utzon, 1948.
MIDDLE Glass tumblers, with J Utzon, awarded second prize in a Nordic competition held in Finland in 1950.
BOTTOM "Le Commerce", competition entry with J Utzon for the Gothenburg School of Business, 1948.

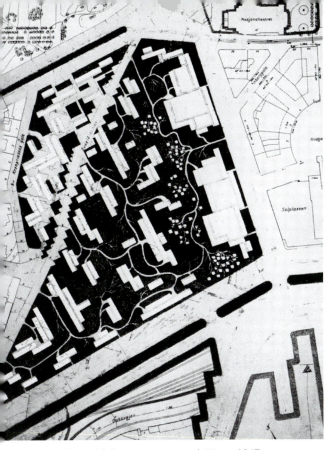

LEFT "Vestre Vika", competition entry with J Utzon, 1947.
RIGHT Jørn Utzon, and Arne and Grete Korsmo at the Bygdøy apartment.

Zaitzow, who had originally worked as a theatre director, was also a painter and scenographer—an inventive "Jack-of-all-trades" who became famous and controversial for his theatre productions throughout Scandinavia. Influenced by Cubism, Functionalism and Art Deco, Zaitzow was known for his modern and highly original visual language.[84] Korsmo and Zaitzow were joint participants in a "playful world".[85] Zaitzow's daughter, the architect and scenographer Tatjana Zaitzow, who was actively involved for many years in puppet theatre, describes accompanying her parents on visits to Planetveien 12. Here she was allowed to build "houses" using the cushions in the living room.[86] Alexey Zaitzow took many photographs of both the Korsmos' work.

7 • ARNE KORSMO AND GRETE PRYTZ

Arne Korsmo received few commissions during the first few years after the war. His work before the war—in particular the houses he had designed for well-to-do clients on the west side of Oslo—had gained him a reputation as an architect for the wealthy. These buildings included the Dammann House (in collaboration with Sverre Aasland) at Havna Allé 15 (now preserved as an outstanding example of Functionalism) and the Stenersen House at Tuengen Allé 10 C (also preserved). Many people thought of Korsmo as a dreamer with a highly artistic temperament—a person who required an exceptional amount of creative freedom. As such, he was seen as incompatible with Norway's programme for postwar reconstruction, which included an austere housing policy based on social-democratic principles.

However, Korsmo's experience designing objects and furniture, as well as his experiences with exhibition and theatre design, provided him with opportunities to develop professionally in many areas other than architecture. Not least his relationship with Grete Prytz led him to experiment with designs for various everyday items and to see them realised in new contexts.[87]

Grete Prytz had completed a diploma in goldsmithing at the National College of Applied Arts in 1941. Her diploma project was an elegant, modernistic silver coffee service, with black plastic handles and footrings. Grete's father, Jacob Tostrup Prytz, was not only rector of the college, but also head of the goldsmithing department. Since 1913, he had been creative director of the family gold- and silversmithing business, J Tostrup, which had been founded by Grete's (and the author's) great-great-grandfather in 1832. Grete's grandfather was the architect and goldsmith Torolf Prytz. He had secured

the company an international reputation by exhibiting at the World Fairs in St Louis in 1898 and in Paris in 1900, where he won a Grand Prix for his "*plique-à-jour*" enamel work. Torolf Prytz had been responsible for modernising the production of silverware in Norway, and was one of the architects responsible for the company's new headquarters, Tostrupgården, which was erected between 1896 and 1898. This building still stands opposite the Norwegian Parliament in the centre of Oslo, although both it and the family business were sold in the autumn of 1984.[88] Torolf's son, and Grete's father, Jacob Tostrup Prytz also became a goldsmith and was active in the Applied Arts Movement both nationally and internationally. From 1918 until 1948 he led the newly established Norwegian Applied Arts Association, and he exhibited his own work in several major exhibitions. Under his creative leadership, the company of J Tostrup focused strongly on research and design. This was evidenced by the establishment, in 1922, of a separate department for modern design known as "Tostrup's Drawing Office". Grete's father had extensive contact with Nordic colleagues, not least with the Svenska Slöjdföreningen (Swedish Applied Arts Association) and its leader, the art historian Gregor Paulsson, who was the author of the Swedish four-volume *World History of Art* and the originator of the phrase "more beautiful everyday things". Paulsson was in overall charge of the 1930 Stockholm Exhibition, which is often described—in particular due to the elegant buildings designed by the architect Gunnar Asplund—as the breakthrough for Modernism and Functionalism in Nordic architecture. Arne Korsmo often talked about these buildings and showed pictures of them.

OPPOSITE TOP Coffee service, diploma project by Grete Prytz, 1941.
OPPOSITE BOTTOM Tostrupgården, 25 Karl Johans Gate.
OPPOSITE RIGHT Grete Prytz Korsmo at work.

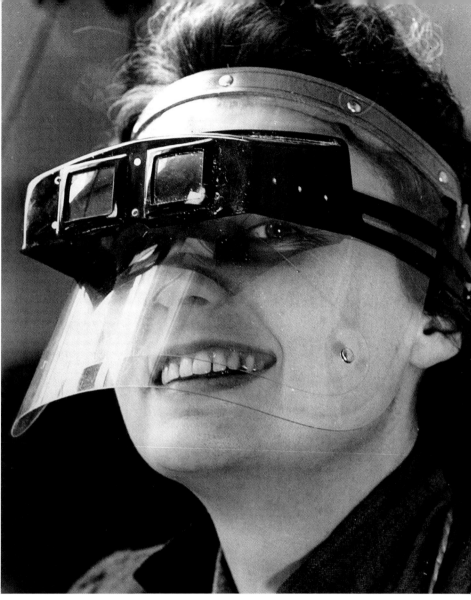

Guests were always welcome at the Prytz family home at Villaveien 25 (now Apalveien 42) in the Blindern neighbourhood of Oslo; even as a child Grete had already met many leading figures in the worlds of architecture and design, including Alvar Aalto and Gregor Paulsson. When Arne Korsmo set up home in 1928 with his first wife, Aase Thiis, at Lille Frøens Vei 14, he was living only a few hundred metres from Grete's childhood home. Five years later, Arne and Aase Korsmo moved with their daughter Nora to the first floor of a house designed by Korsmo at Havna Allé 12. Aase's father, Karl Sivertsen Thiis, lived on the ground floor.[89]

As a child, Grete Prytz often passed Havna Allé on her way to school at Vinderen. She often visited

her paternal grandparents at their home, "Solhaugen", at Ivar Aasens Vei 14. Alternatively she could visit her maternal grandparents, the Juels, at their large property "Lønnhaugen" a little further west in Vinderen.[90] Grete enjoyed a privileged childhood, with both her parents coming from well-to-do families that owned large houses and other property.

Arne Korsmo grew up in Oslo, first at Niels Juels Gate 3 in the Skillebekk neighbourhood and later at Sorgenfrigaten 37 in the Majorstuen neighbourhood, both near the centre of the city. Arne, who was the eldest child of Emil and Aagot Jacobine Korsmo, had one sister, Bergljot, who was four years younger. At that time his father was in charge of the farming and rural estates owned by the city. This included the land belonging to Frogner Manor (Frogner Hovedgård), which Arne remembered visiting frequently with his father.

Although Emil Korsmo had never taken the university entrance examination (*examen artium*), he attended the courses in botany at the University of Kristiania (now Oslo) from 1911 to 1913. As a result he obtained a post as a governmental adviser in the Ministry of Agriculture.

He had been carrying out innovative research in herbology since 1888, and in 1920—the same year that Arne passed his university entrance examination—was appointed professor at the Agricultural College of Norway. Originally there was talk of Arne following his father into agriculture and he undertook practical work in one of the college's muck cellars. Partly due to his problems with asthma, however, Arne decided to apply to the Norwegian Institute of Technology (NTH) in Trondheim. At NTH he initially studied civil engineering, before transferring to the Faculty of Architecture, from which he graduated in 1926.

OPPOSITE TOP LEFT Arne Korsmo, early self-portrait.
OPPOSITE RIGHT Arne Korsmo's family circa 1937. From left, his sister Bergljot, her husband Trygve Mørdre, Aase (Thiis) Korsmo, Arne and Aase's daughter Nora, Arne Korsmo, and his parents Aagot and Emil Korsmo.
OPPOSITE BOTTOM Arne Korsmo with his father, Emil.
ABOVE Competition entry for Norway's pavilion at the Paris World Fair, 1936.

The Paris World Fair and wartime exile

Grete was 17 years younger than Arne. She met him for the first time at the Paris World Fair in 1937, which she was visiting with her father and her brother Torolf. Four years Grete's senior, Torolf was already well on his way to completing his goldsmithing training. Grete was 20 and was spending the year living with a family in Normandy. The objective was for her to learn French, but she also spent time horse-riding and practised fencing. Grete's father was chairman of the Norwegian committee for the World Fair. At the exhibition in Paris, he introduced a collection of enamel pieces, some of which were awarded the highest honour of a Grand Prix. Grete travelled to Paris to meet her father and brother—and also of course to see the World Fair. Arne Korsmo was in Paris as co-designer of the Norwegian pavilion. Once back in Oslo, Grete completed her goldsmithing training and worked more-or-less as a secretary for her father at the family firm. By that time the war had come to Norway. After having been involved in illegal

LEFT Promotional brochure for the "Korsmo" cutlery set signed by Gunnar S Gundersen, 1954.
RIGHT Double die for pressing spoons for the "Korsmo" cutlery set.
OPPOSITE TOP Candelabra in silver with enamel by Grete and Arne Korsmo, 1951.
OPPOSITE BOTTOM Unrealised project for a new Tostrupgård building.

activities during the German occupation of Norway, in 1943 Grete fled on skis over the border to Sweden. In Stockholm she found work as a shorthand typist at the Legal Office of the Norwegian legation.

In 1944, Arne Korsmo had arrived in Stockholm and found work at Hedqvist's architecture practice, and on 30 April 1945 (a few days before Germany capitulated and the war ended) Grete Prytz and Arne Korsmo married in Stockholm. To the astonishment of their friends and colleagues, they cycled during their lunch break to the district judge, were married in haste and then cycled back to work. The time spent in Stockholm offered many interesting experiences and new friendships. In particular, their friendship with Lis and Jørn Utzon was to be important for their work in later years. Back in

Oslo they rented a studio apartment in St Olavs Gate, the street where the National College of Applied Arts was located. Arne was working at the college, and the apartment was also very close to the J Tostrup workshop, where Grete was working.

Broad-based productivity

As time went on, Arne Korsmo also became more involved in work for the Prytz family's business. His brother-in-law Torolf Prytz had now become general manager and both he and his father supported Arne and Grete Korsmo's creative activities. Among other ventures, the business focused on developing "Korsmo", a 21-piece silver-plated cutlery set. Both Arne and Grete worked on the distinctively designed pieces between 1947 and 1954. Designed to be mass-produced, the pieces reflected the application of principles for streamlining the manufacturing process. Each piece was stamped out of a one mm-thick piece of sheet metal and then pressed in a double die to achieve the desired degree of stiffness and strength. In addition, the curvilinear design gave the piece elegance and ornament. As Arne described the process in his idiosyncratic style:

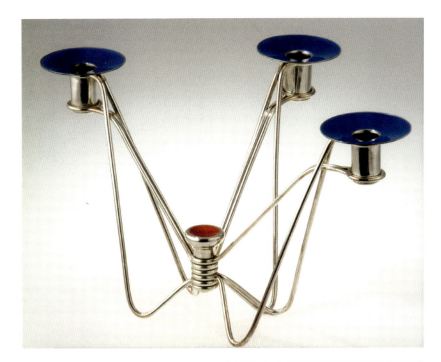

> To achieve a controlled use of silver for a piece of cutlery, one must determine the most economical way to proceed. Silver molecules may bond in different ways that will make the metal either more malleable or stiffer. By pressing a one mm-thick silver sheet in a double die, one can form the individual pieces of cutlery with a single hammer blow, except for the knife, which has a steel blade joined to the silver handle. [...] What we must endeavour to achieve is to develop the ability to shape [items] with a machine as a natural tool, so that the mass-produced product becomes what it should be: the highest expression of logical and sensory quality. This does not reduce the value of the hand—that which, when building the models, articulated the first expression of the concept and formed the basis for the repetitive result.[91]

The cost implications, combined with post-war restrictions on the use of silver, meant that the cutlery was produced in electro-plated nickel silver, rather than pure silver.[92] Stainless steel was considered as an alternative, but the two designers wanted the unique qualities of silver: the softer, deeper lustre that is so different from stainless steel. Another factor was that stainless steel did not fit into the profile of a gold- and silversmithing business. Form and material work together, and silver suits the elegance of the form. At the same time, the pressed shape was a particularly appropriate response to modern ideas about function, in relation both to production and to the finished product. In the case of the fork, for example, the number of operations required for the pressing was reduced to two, as opposed to the usual number of eight.[93] In addition, the forks and spoons can be stacked for compact storage. Although Arne

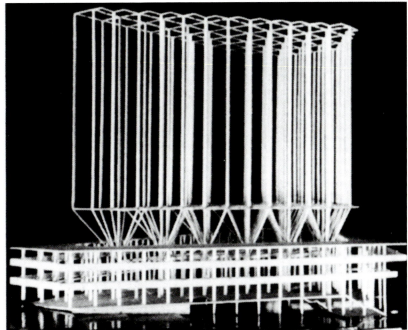

Events and highlights

As mentioned previously, Arne Korsmo obtained few architectural commissions after the war and lamented that he was no longer "used" as an architect.[94] Nevertheless, in the early 1950s the Korsmos were a particularly productive team in many other fields. While Grete produced many enamel pieces in which she experimented with techniques and formats, Arne devoted a great deal of time to teaching. In addition he collaborated with members of PAGON on competition entries and projects, and with Norberg-Schulz as his assistant he designed the Alfredheim Girls' Home in Oslo. Korsmo created detailed plans for a project to build a new Tostrupgård (the Tostrup company's headquarters) opposite the Norwegian Parliament building in Oslo. The proposed building was distinctly innovative, both in design and construction, and was never realised. The project encountered strong opposition from the company's lawyers.[95] This was also the period when the initial planning for the houses in Planetveien got underway.

At the ninth CIAM congress in Aix-en-Provence in the summer of 1953, the theme was 'habitation'. This was intended as an homage to Le Corbusier and his famous concept of the 'habitat'. The CIAM network was extremely important for Korsmo, and by now Grete had become something of an unofficial delegate to its international conferences. She later described the concluding party of the congress, which took the form of a nocturnal fete on the rooftop terrace of Le Corbusier's apartment block in Marseilles, which was lit for the occasion like a beacon.[96]

In the autumn of the same year, the Korsmos each exhibited work at Galerie Artek in Helsinki. Grete showed a varied range of silver and enamel pieces, while Arne displayed examples of his architectural work and furniture. The exhibition was a major event for the couple, as well as being one of the "highlights of the autumn" for the design community in Helsinki.[97] Grete had first met her Finnish friend Maire Gullichsen at the Paris World Fair in 1937. Maire Gullichsen was an art collector and a leading member of the cultural elite—an enthusiastic advocate for modern art, architecture

LEFT From the Milan Triennale, 1954.
OPPOSITE Grete and Arne Korsmo at the opening of their Helskinki exhibition in 1953.

Korsmo received the credit, the cutlery service was the result of close collaboration with Grete and her brother, Torolf. Although Arne was very likely a driving force in the design, Grete undoubtedly had a deeper knowledge of techniques for making silver objects and drawing up designs before production. She was very experimental in her approach and completely familiar with modernistic design ideals and principles.

Collaborations between the couple resulted in further silver objects, including a three-branched candelabra in silver and enamel, and a silver jug with an ergonomic handle in black or transparent plastic, which was available off-the-shelf in two sizes. These objects are remarkable for their extremely simple yet elegant designs. Often daringly asymmetrical, with straight lines and curving forms, the pieces combine silver with innovative materials such as transparent acrylic, as well as coloured enamel.

and design.[98] Together with Aino and Alvar Aalto, and the journalist Nils-Gustav Hahl, she founded the design company Artek. Maire's husband, Harry Gullichsen, was Norwegian and the Korsmos visited them several times at their world-famous home, Villa Mairea, which Alvar Aalto had designed for them at Noormarkku, a few miles inland from the Gulf of Bothnia in western Finland.

During the same period, Grete and Arne Korsmo were working towards the exhibition Design in Scandinavia, which had been planned at the major Nordic applied arts congresses between 1946 and 1954. The Korsmos were a natural choice to participate in this exhibition. The exhibition opened in Richmond, Virginia in January 1954 and then toured until 1957 to 24 venues on the North American continent.

1954 was a particularly intense and eventful year. The house in Planetveien was to be built, and a number of details had to be resolved and drawn up.[99] At the same time both Korsmos were working at full capacity on Norway's contribution to the important international Triennale design fair in Milan. Arne Korsmo had been appointed architect for the Norwegian section of the exhibition in the spring, and Grete began work on her exhibits in the summer. The exhibition opened on 28 August and ran until 15 November. Gunnar S Gundersen participated in the design and choice of colours for the exhibition and also contributed four abstract paintings that were hung on the back wall.

Korsmo's exhibition architecture made the Norwegian section quite unique—a refined modern framework for the varied objects on display; a pavilion within the pavilion with elegantly mounted shelves and tables, all of which were a part of the rhythmically divided sections—modules—on the floor, walls and ceiling. Korsmo was awarded a Grand Prix, the highest award possible at the Triennale, for his exhibition architecture. Grete exhibited 12 enamel pieces, including a majestic blue dish 70 cm in diameter that she had fired at the Emaljeverket factory in Oslo, which usually fired enamelled bathtubs.[100] Grete was also awarded a Grand Prix for her work. In addition the couple were awarded two gold medals, one for the

"Korsmo" cutlery set and one for an appetizer dish that was exhibited on the "herring table" in the Norwegian section. In addition to their participation in a number of other exhibitions in the period, the couple were represented at the major Nordic H-55 exhibition in Helsingborg in the summer of 1955; as was often the case, they collaborated on this exhibition with Gunnar S Gundersen.

The Korsmos moved into Planetveien 12 in the early winter of 1955, before the interior was completely finished. Not long afterwards, in the autumn of 1956, Arne Korsmo took up a professorship at the Department for Architectural Design II at the Norwegian Institute of Technology (NTH) in Trondheim. He had applied unsuccessfully for this position in 1948, but was successful this time. The opportunity had arisen because the incumbent professor, the architect Odd Brochmann, had resigned in order to move to Copenhagen. Grete decided not to move to Trondheim. She wanted to live in Oslo and continue with her activities at their live-work home in Planetveien and at the family goldsmithing business.

Together—and apart

In Trondheim, Korsmo had the opportunity to develop a completely new, Bauhaus-inspired curriculum from the ground up, since "his" department had primary responsibility for teaching first- and second-year students.

Architecture was Korsmo's true area of expertise and he now had the chance to make it the focus of his activities. He was able to use his experiences with other fields of design, which he had had the opportunity to cultivate at the Department of Timber-based Design in Oslo and with the gold- and silversmithing company J Tostrup, to supplement and enhance his architecture teaching. The professorship also strengthened Korsmo's international position and network. Initially he stayed at the Britannia Hotel, but after a while he found a small apartment in a 1930s apartment block known as "Vestråt" in Elvegaten, a street near the city centre.[101] Grete came to Trondheim frequently on long and short visits, while Arne was likewise frequently at Planetveien.

Grete was herself experiencing a flourishing phase of her creative activity: she was a key member of staff at her family company, and was also busy developing high-quality enamels in collaboration with the Norwegian Industrial Research Institute, where her brother-in-law was a civil engineer. Involved in this collaboration was Cathrineholm AS, a company that manufactured enamelled steel products. She had also embarked on a collaboration with the Italian designer and glass artist Paolo Venini and his glass factory on the Venetian island of Murano.

Grete and Arne Korsmo continued to collaborate after Arne moved to Trondheim in 1956, not least through their participation in exhibitions in both Norway and abroad. At the Triennale in Milan in 1957, Arne won a gold medal for exhibition architecture, while Grete won a gold medal for her original enamel pieces, as well as for her Cathrineholm products. Once again Gunnar S Gundersen contributed in various ways to the creation of a complete artistic concept for the Norwegian section.

In 1960, the Korsmos divorced. In 1965, Arne married for the third time, this time to the architect Hanne Refsdal, with whom he had two daughters (Anne Lin, born 1965 and Marie, born 1966). But Grete and Arne remained friends and Arne often stayed at Planetveien when he was visiting Oslo. According to Hanne Refsdal, their daughter Anne Lin took her first steps on the carpet in the living room there.[102] Korsmo also continued to receive commissions from J Tostrup for the rest of his life. While working as Korsmo's assistant in the spring of 1968, I designed a new entrance for the J Tostrup shop in Karl Johans Gate in connection with a refurbishment of the company's premises.

In 1971, Grete married Sverre Kittelsen, taking his surname in addition to hers.[103] Her career would continue to develop such that she is now considered one of the foremost Nordic designers, having had significant influence on Norwegian applied arts and design from the era of Scandinavian Design (1945–1965) to the present day.

The results of Grete and Arne Korsmo's collaborations and activities in the years they lived together are remarkable for their diversity and quality. Their working relationship imbued their work with an intensity—and a

A Christmas display window for J Tostrup, the gold- and silversmithing firm.

mutual productivity—that resulted in high points for each of their exceptional careers. Together—and apart—they created ground-breaking works in the fields of design and architecture. Their work is characterised by its great breadth and originality. The way in which Grete and Arne Korsmo mutually enriched each other's creative achievement is a phenomenon they shared with other couples where both partners have been independent practitioners in creative fields.[104] Such relationships may of course involve self-denial and imbalances, and the "working constellation" may be affected by entrenched gender stereotypes—for example, the woman's achievement may be perceived as less important than the man's.

In the case of the Korsmos, however, the result was an astounding breadth, strength and intensity. For his part, Arne, the architect, had a unique opportunity to use his talents in the fields of the applied arts, silversmithing and exhibition design. Meanwhile Grete, the goldsmith and enamel artist, was stimulated to expand beyond her original field to work with mass production and to use modern materials such as plastic and glass. Through her collaborations with Korsmo and with Gundersen, she was able to expand the repertoire of architectural and artistic references that she could employ when working with objects. In this way she was able to extend her artistic sphere of operations. The Korsmos' creative endeavours were set against their backgrounds in different design disciplines. They were co-participants in a complete design process wherein each individual's contribution enhanced the quality of the final result.

Arne Korsmo died in 1968 while on a journey on which Grete was one of his companions. The destination was Peru, where both were to participate in an international crafts congress. Korsmo had looked forward to seeing the magnificent Inca ruins at Machu Picchu. As Hanne Refsdal told me in 2007, "It was his lifelong dream."[105] The ruins lie high in the Andes, a few hours from the town of Cuzco. Cuzco lies about 3,400 m above sea-level, while Machu Picchu is about 2,500 m above sea-level, so the trip was risky for Korsmo. Because he had had three-quarters of one lung removed, he often had breathing problems even at 1,000 m above sea-level. He collapsed at the entrance to the ruined city and died of pneumonia in hospital in Lima on 29 August.

It is unclear how Arne Korsmo and Christian Norberg-Schulz came into contact with the owner of the land in Planetveien. Due to his reduced lung capacity and asthma, Korsmo was eager to live closer to nature and preferably at a slightly higher altitude, where the air was fresher.[106] Christian Norberg-Schulz was young and relatively newly qualified as an architect when the two men embarked on their joint project. For both of them it represented an opportunity to build contemporary homes for their own use, while also building something completely new and experimental in some of the best surroundings in Oslo.

At the time there were only a few other houses in the sparsely populated neighbourhood. The project required the merger of two land units (cadastral unit no. 41, property units nos. 419 and 420), which would then be subdivided into three plots. The addresses allocated to these plots were, respectively, Planetveien 10, 12 and 14. The arrangement was that the landowner, the company manager J H Nordlie, would have one of the houses, with Norberg-Schulz and Korsmo each taking one of the remaining plots. Official consent to the merger of the two units of land was granted on 13 May 1954. In addition to planning his own house at no. 14, Norberg-Schulz took on most of the work of planning Nordlie's house at no.10.

The application for building consent for the three houses was dated 13 March 1952, prior to Norberg-Schulz's departure for the United States. When the application was put out for public consultation, five neighbours lodged objections. These neighbours disliked the idea of a row of attached houses so close to the forest and they stated in forthright language that the character of the area required development to be restricted to free-standing houses on large forested plots.[107] One objection compared the total length of the row of houses (50 m) to the length of the new Oslo City Hall. These objections caused some delay to the application process. Finally, however, the City Council decided to allow "the row of attached houses to be constructed on the property", adding that "The objecting neighbours have been informed of this [decision]."[108]

The housing experiment—in particular no.12—takes shape

Right from the start, the attached houses were intended to be experimental housing. The planning application, under "Special particulars", described the project as "Experimental building with no basement, but with underfloor heating. Construction using standard elements, so that the same dwelling may be adapted for different and varying requirements."[109] On 18 March 1953, the city's building authority resolved:

The house is deemed to constitute experimental housing for the purposes of testing new materials, constructions and types of dwelling. The building authority will not object to the approval in general terms of the planning application and attached drawings dated 13 March 1953, subject to such conditions as may be imposed by the city planning authority, the health authority, the fire authority and building control [...] There can be no assumption that electrical heating will be provided by Oslo Lysverker [the municipal electricity supplier].[110]

One member of the authority voted against approving the application on the grounds that: "The glass surface will not provide adequate protection against cold and

Interior perspective, sketch.

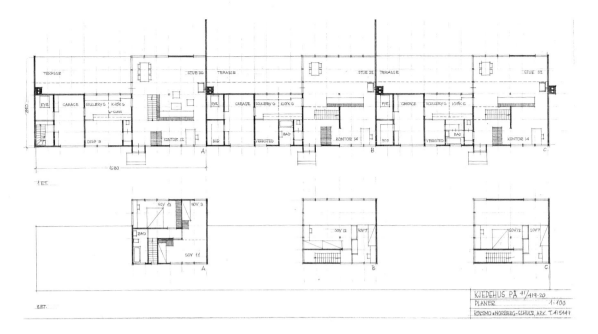

Early plans for the row of attached houses, undated.

heat." There was a certain amount of correspondence with the municipal health and fire authorities before final approval was granted. Among other things, the health authority recommended the addition of a cellar or other room for the storage of potatoes, preserved foods, etc..[111] Requirements were also imposed regarding the inclusion of a draught lobby for each unit. Another source of problems was fire separation between the houses, and fire safety in general, due to the size of the houses' overall footprint (340 m²) and the fact that the garages were sandwiched between houses with adjoining walls.

Christian Norberg-Schulz was in the United States from July 1952 until May 1953. Given the state of communications at that time, it is unlikely that he was participating actively in the project during this period. Soon after he returned to Norway, however, he wrote a letter, dated 30 June 1953, to the Oslo Fire Department concerning the fire separation walls between houses A, B and C.[112]

A body of correspondence exists between municipal departments, the architect and various consulting engineers concerning the heating system and the steel structure. In this regard it is possible to trace changes in Korsmo's design subsequent to the initial planning application. Initially, all three houses had been designed with similar floor plans. In other words, the Korsmos' house resembled Norberg-Schulz's, with a column in the middle of the living room and secondary rooms between the living room and the wall closest to the road. A proposal to the building authority, accompanied by new plans, submitted on 13 March 1953 stated that: "The balcony in the living room in House B (no.12) shall be suspended from a steel beam." This suggests that Korsmo, in the winter of 1953, had not yet arrived at his final design, but was still envisioning the first floor as a balcony or mezzanine. An axonometric drawing of the steel structure dated 3 January 1953 is stamped as having been received by building control on 5 February 1954. This shows central support beams with a dimension of I–30 spanning the distance between the external walls, with the result that the Korsmos' living room was free of columns.[113]

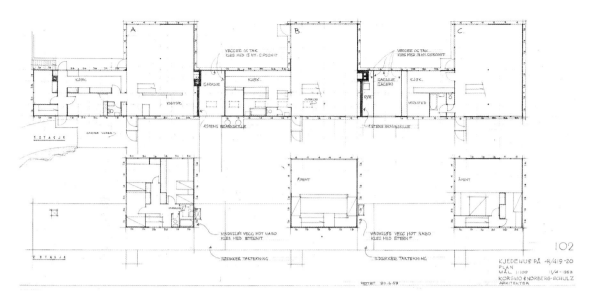

Plans dated 11 April 1953. no.12 has no central column in the living room and the upper floor is a mezzanine over the eastern end of the living room.

In any event, at some point Korsmo adopted the solution that was actually built, with the large column-free living room and the kitchen and entrance lobby in the form presented earlier. Korsmo had probably already arrived at this solution when the architect Odd Kjeld Østbye created his models of different furnishing configurations in the living room for the exhibition in Helsinki in the autumn of 1953. The upper floor fills the volume within the external walls, and the final drawings to be submitted, dated 13 April 1954, also show the upper floor as subdivided into four rooms: two bedrooms, an office and a wardrobe (the latter located where the dressing/guest room is today). According to Prytz Kittelsen, evidence of this type of floor plan was essential for obtaining the building loan. These new drawings, which were stamped as approved on 20 May, were "not to be used on the building site before they have been stamped as approved by the rationing office for building materials".

Prytz Kittelsen often told me that "Arne 'solved the house' on a concert programme while we were at a concert in the Aula [the main Oslo concert hall]." Korsmo doodled and sketched almost constantly, and it is certainly likely that he began seriously to work out his designs for the house following a final "breakthrough", which may well have occurred as he sketched on a concert programme. Most of the working drawings are dated sequentially through the remainder of 1954, although a number of schedules and details are dated after the Korsmos moved into no.12 in 1955.

Dispensation from the "Regulations concerning house-building within urban areas"

The attached houses in Planetveien were featured soon after completion in the Norwegian architectural journal *Byggekunst*, as well as in several foreign journals, such as *The Architectural Review* (UK), *Werk* (Switzerland) and *Architettura* (Italy). As time has gone by, the houses have gained iconic status in the history of Norwegian architecture. They represent a highly valued heritage from 1950s modernism and are continually referred to by

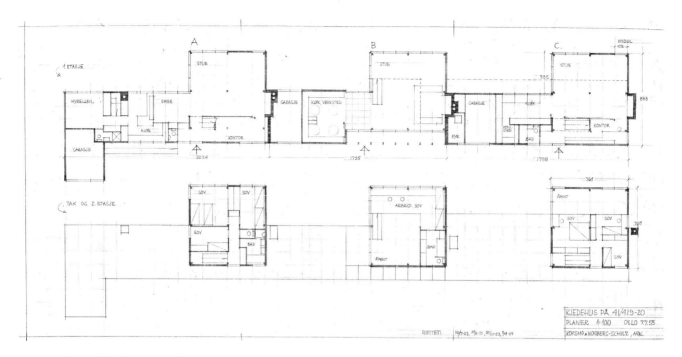

Plans dated 7 July 1953. Here the upper floor is a mezzanine over the western end of the living room.

official bodies and in the teaching of architecture students. In 2007, the Norwegian newspaper *Morgenbladet* further confirmed their status when it included the attached houses, in particular Korsmo's house, in its list of the 12 most significant post-war buildings in Norway.[114] Even further confirmation was granted when Oslo's Cultural Heritage Management Office proposed Planetveien 12 for listing as a protected building.

Among Norwegian architectural circles in the 1950s, however, Korsmo's house had a more mixed reception. The house's "exotic" materials and costly construction processes were provocative. Many architects at that time were slaving away at more prosaic, but extremely necessary, assignments. Norway was in a period of reconstruction and housebuilding in which the ability to tackle everyday problems was hampered by rationing and tough regulation. The majority of architects were stuck with making the best of a difficult situation. The director of the Oslo Housing Department described the situation as follows:

After the war, one's objective was to build dwellings with three rooms and a kitchen, which equated to an apartment of approx. 80 m^2 [....] In order to comply with its policy to build as many apartments as possible while keeping the consumption of materials and labour to a minimum, the Ministry has in general had to refuse permission to developers to build [units] larger than 80 m^2, has encouraged the use of constructions that are economical with timber and has prohibited the building of detached houses within towns and in densely populated areas. This leaves architects and developers little room for manoeuvre.[115]

Due to the incorporation into Oslo in 1948 of the municipality of Aker, which included Vettakollen, the Regulation concerning housebuilding in urban areas applied to Planetveien. According to the Regulation's rules governing semi-detached houses and row houses with two complete storeys, which came under the category "Wooden houses", the maximum permissible ground

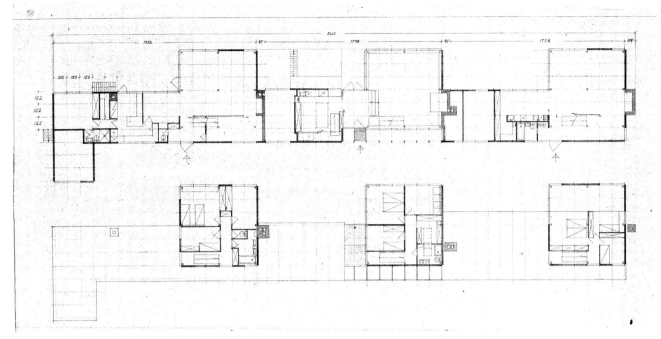

Plans showing the upper floor divided into several bedrooms.

floor area was 40 m² (net internal area) and 45 m² (gross external area), for a one-and-a-half-storey house. Korsmo's house had a gross external ground floor area of approximately 107 m², including the garage which is 15 m².[116] In other words, the ground floor area was more than double the post-war norm.

As a general rule, using space as an office or for similar purposes did not allow any increase in the permitted ground floor area. Using space in the house as a workplace did, however, provide grounds for seeking a dispensation, and well-reasoned applications were often successful.[117] The "live-work" home at Planetveien 12 exploited this possibility to the full.

So-called experimental houses were also a building category for which permission could be granted to exceed prevailing restrictions on materials.[118] "Experimental housing—three attached houses" was the title Korsmo gave to his application to Oslo's building authority in March 1953. Among other things, the application highlighted the fact that "the building shall be constructed of profiled steel rails that will be welded together". In addition the authority was informed that the architect Korsmo wishes to use the glass facade to carry out heating-related experiments. Tests are to be carried out inside the house using different blinds, coloured plastic screens and curtains in order to investigate the possibilities for secondary heat transfer at different times of day.[119]

During the years after the war, both labour and timber were in short supply. Official policy was to encourage building with wood-saving, lightweight structures that used 2" x 4" (48 x 98 mm) timber and new insulating and cladding materials instead of the traditional two-layer panelling. Not least, the authorities wanted to discourage construction with logs. The attached houses in Planetveien complied with these requirements, but went significantly further towards experimental and "un-Norwegian" architecture than the examples recommended by the Housing Department.

A provocative house

The PAGON member PAM Mellbye discussed the problems associated with post-war building restrictions in his article "Can we live happily in 80–90 m²?" In the article he referred to the situation in the United States and to open floor plans and the flexibility offered by fixed and moveable elements in the dwelling. He concluded that "100 m², or perhaps a little smaller, could cover the vast majority of families' requirements".[120]

The book *Small Nordic Houses*, which was published in 1958 on the occasion of Nordic Architecture Day VII in Oslo, presents around 40 newly built small houses in Norway.[121] The houses of several PAGON members are presented here, with one or two pages devoted to each. Remarkably, however, Korsmo's house is not included. In his introduction to the section containing the Norwegian houses, the young architect Kjell Lund maintains that "the architecture of small houses is an art of moderation and limitation", but also "to a particular degree the object of experiment".[122] Lund seeks new ideas and visionary solutions where:

> The daring and unusual are cultivated to something more than tedious effect, and where large and small are as they are, without a hint of exhibitionism. A particular characteristic of small-house architecture in recent times is the so-called 'open floor plan', with the possibilities offered by new glass products for greater contact with nature and our surroundings.[123]

A small photograph of Planetveien 12 in the margin of this article accompanies Lund's description of Korsmo's newly built house:

> In a country such as Norway, where people were pretty much living in winter dens up until 1955, the year when Professor Arne Korsmo was the first person since the last Ice Age to crawl out and squint at the sun through his glass prisms on Vettakollen, these trends have been extremely provocative. For many of us, Korsmo's house has been a continuing source of unease that we return to again and again in an attempt to take note of our reaction to it. The indisputable value of the house as a housing experiment lies primarily not in the expression it gives to a relatively unconventional way of organising one's home, but in the way it positions one in a relationship with nature that was previously unknown. The real meaning of this is something that can ultimately be determined only through a person's own experience, but I would think that it is just as likely to give rise to a liberating proactivity as to further passivity, and that a person's genuine experience of nature is not necessarily deepened simply because he or she is observing nature either in or from a showcase—all things considered.[124]

In the course of the same year, the unease that Lund experienced in his encounter with Korsmo's house is expressed in his article about houses and glass in the Norwegian architecture journal *Byggekunst*:

> A couple of years ago, an attached house in Oslo with external walls of glass attracted an enormous amount of attention and is still considered an extremely sophisticated expression of the prevailing architectural views of our times. I have tried many times to discover what this house actually represents and what it really means. You may feel very provoked by the house and want to throw stones. But that is not something you would do at this time, when you're still not certain where you stand on the issue. The house is reminiscent of a soap bubble and also has a soap bubble's fragile beauty. One puff of wind—and the bubble bursts.[125]

Lund's ambivalence and doubt reflected a widespread attitude among leading Norwegian architects at the time: while renewal and progress were express goals, and there was willingness for the new architecture to be inspired by international examples, this should be accomplished in a way that also linked it to Norwegian architectural traditions. According to Lund, a synthesis of intellect and emotion had to form the basis of the new architecture, in which natural materials should be preferred to those of a synthetic nature. The latter were considered to have disturbing psychological effects. In

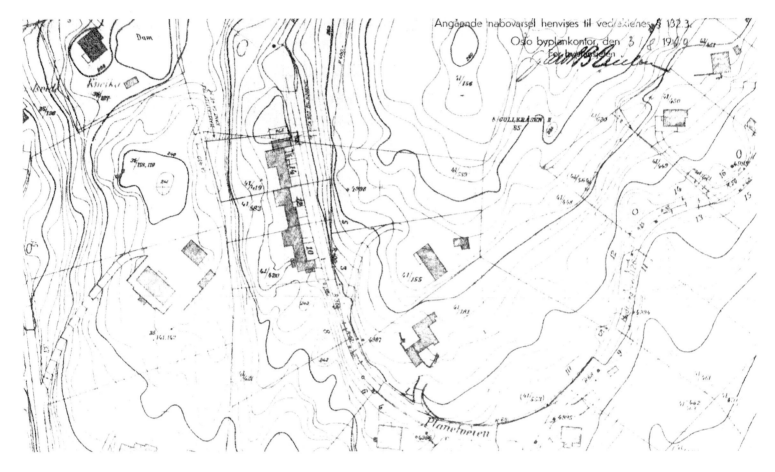

Location map from a planning application for an extension to no. 14 Planetveien, 1969.

this respect Lund's thinking conforms with the so-called Knutsen school, named after the architect Knut Knutsen, who was a contemporary of Korsmo's and an important influence in architectural circles at that time in Norway.[126] Knutsen promoted ideas about moderation and advanced the ideal of natural materials, such as brick and wood. He was also concerned with architectural honesty in construction, materials and design. Both camps in Norwegian architectural circles took inspiration from anonymous architecture worldwide, but interpreted it in different ways.

It was not only the architectonic qualities of Korsmo's house in Planetveien that were provocative to his contemporaries, it was also the lifestyle that the architecture implied. In several ways this lifestyle was completely incompatible with the ideals underlying post-war reconstruction. The prevailing housing programme was steeped in the idea of the family—a married couple with two or more children where the mother was a full-time housewife—leading to the construction of housing units with separate rooms and, increasingly, standardised kitchens designed to make the housewife's work easier.

A well-known anecdote about Planetveien 12 relates that Korsmo telephoned the architect Frode Rinnan to invite him to visit the newly finished house. At first Rinnan said nothing, but then he said: "Thank you. I'd like to visit, but please could you get me a decent chair. I'm too old to crawl around on the floor with a cup of tea." Later Rinnan related how Korsmo had indeed bought a "decent chair", to which he had attached a label: "Frode Rinnan's chair".[127]

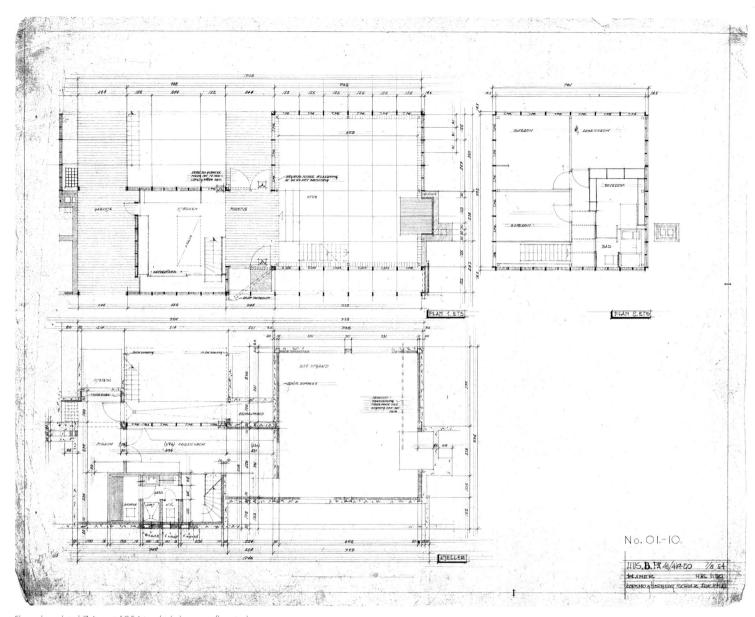

Floor plans dated 7 August 1954 in which the upper floor is shown
as divided into several bedrooms.

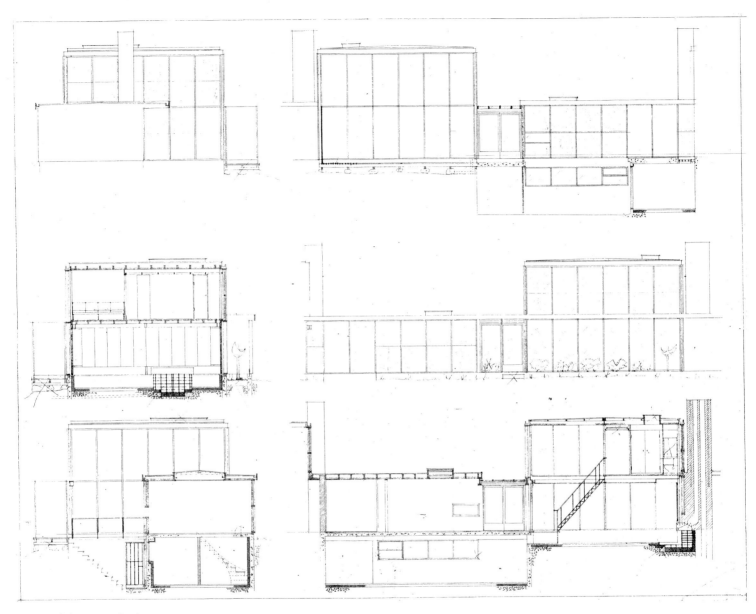

Sections and elevations, undated.

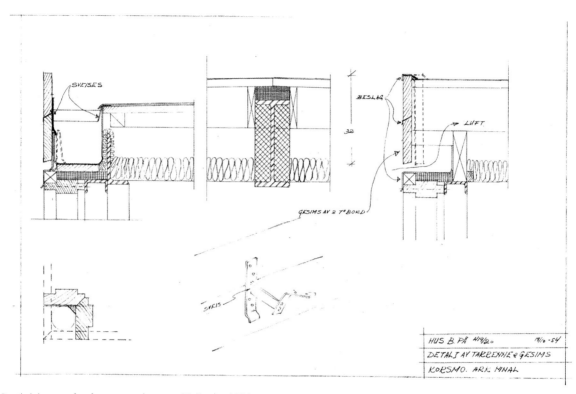

SVEISES

BESLAG

LUFT

32

GESIMS AV 2 7" BORD

SVEIS

HUS B. PÅ 4/4/20   19/10 -54

DETALJ AV TAKRENNE & GESIMS

KORSMO. ARK MNAL

Detailed drawing of roof guttering and casings, 18 October 1954.

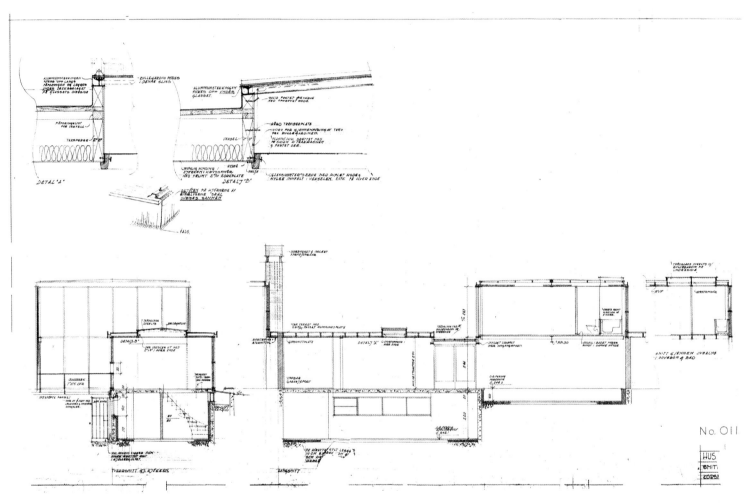

Sections.

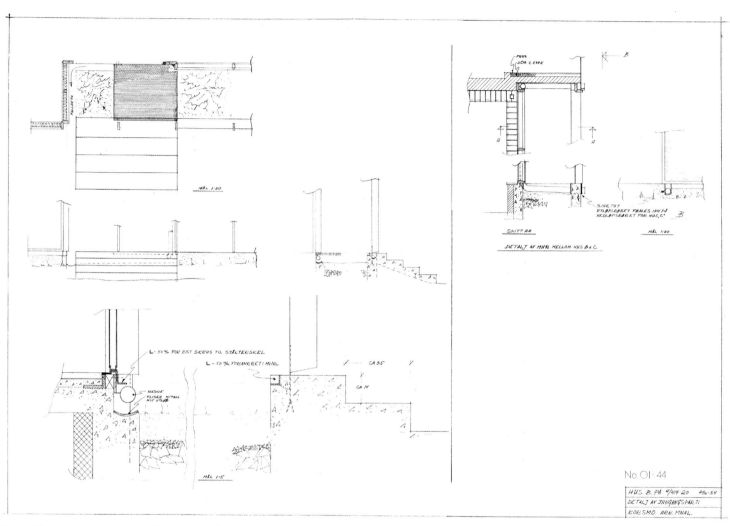

Detailed drawings for the entrance to the house, 21 October 1954.

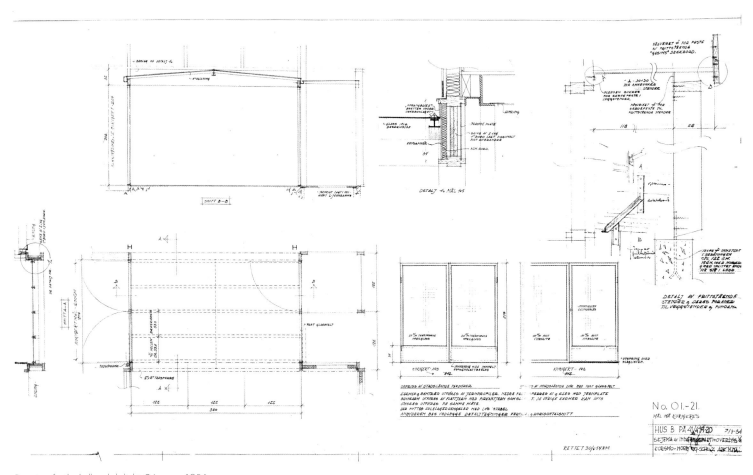

Drawings for the hall and skylight, 9 January 1954.

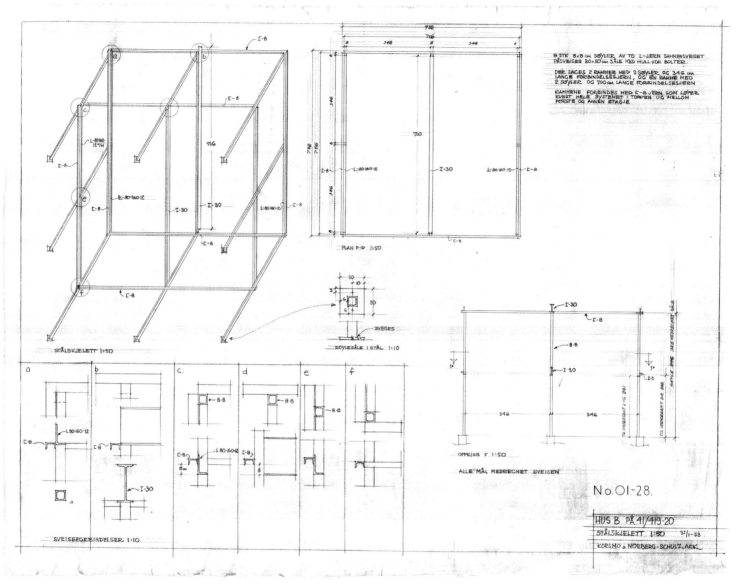

The steel frame, 31 January 1953.

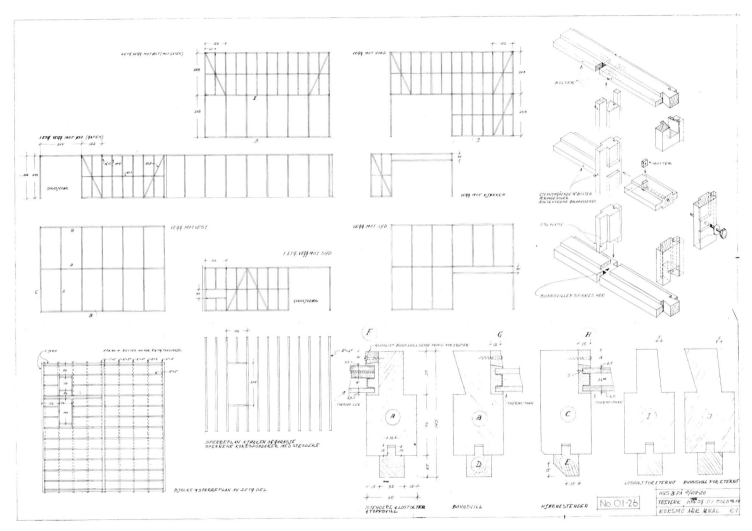

Timber studding, 12 August 1954.

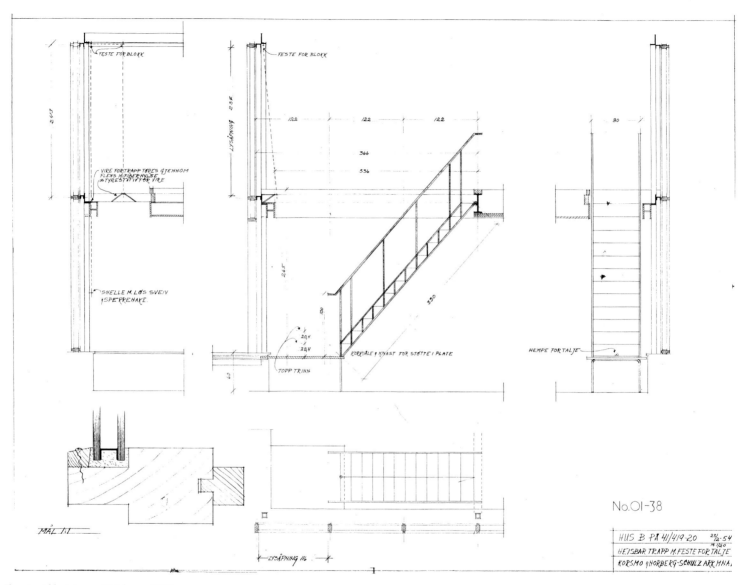

The retractable staircase, 25 February 1954.

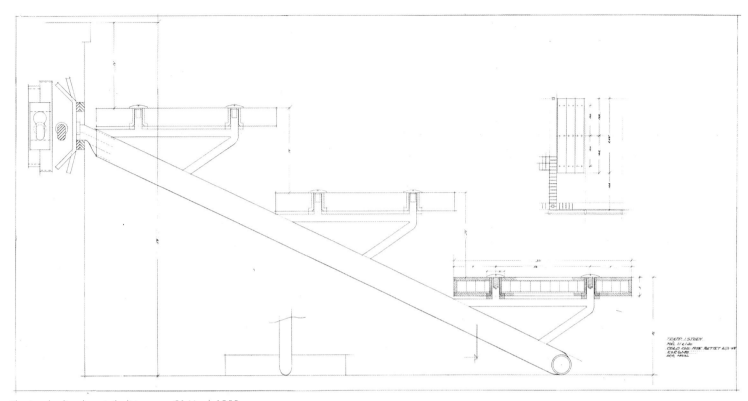

The steps leading down to the living room, 21 March 1955.

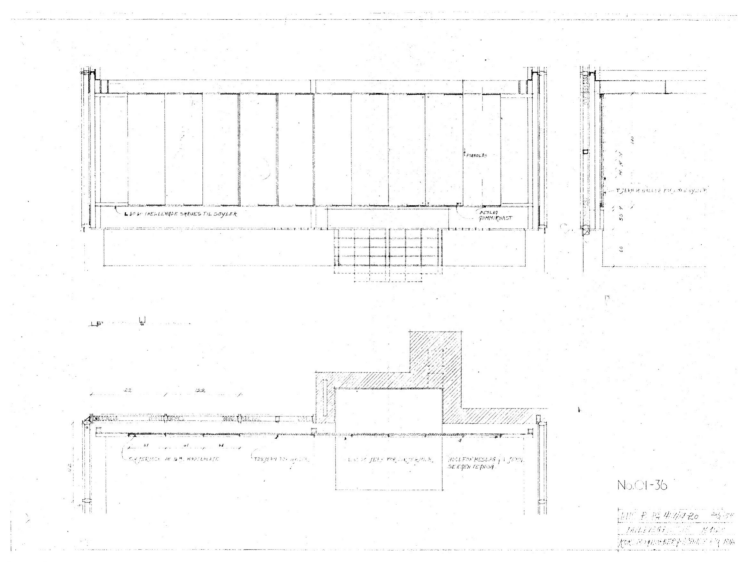

The wall of cupboards with reversible doors, 20 February 1954.

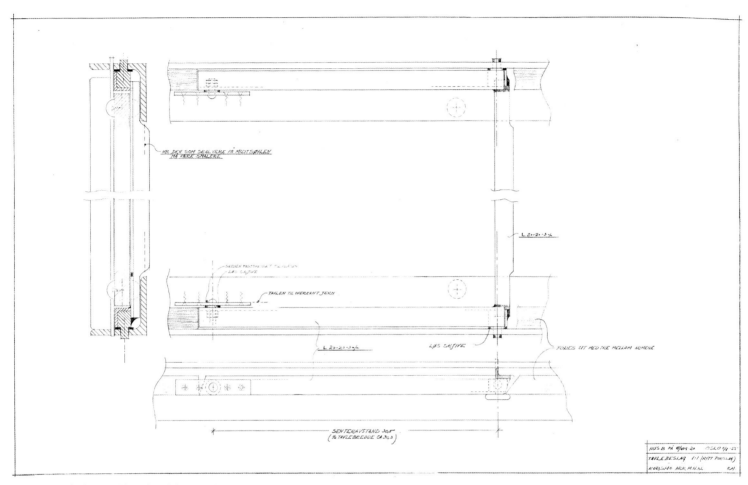

Door mountings for the reversible cupboard doors, 8 July 1955.

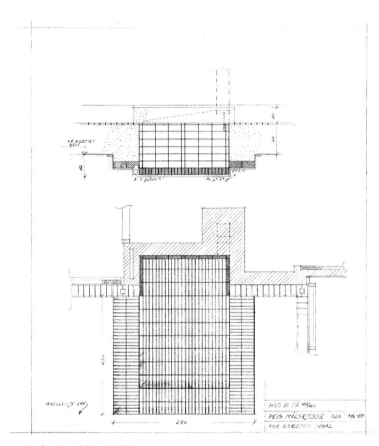

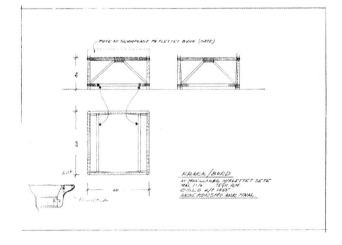

LEFT The fireplace, 30 April 1954.
RIGHT Stool/side table, 2 January 1955.

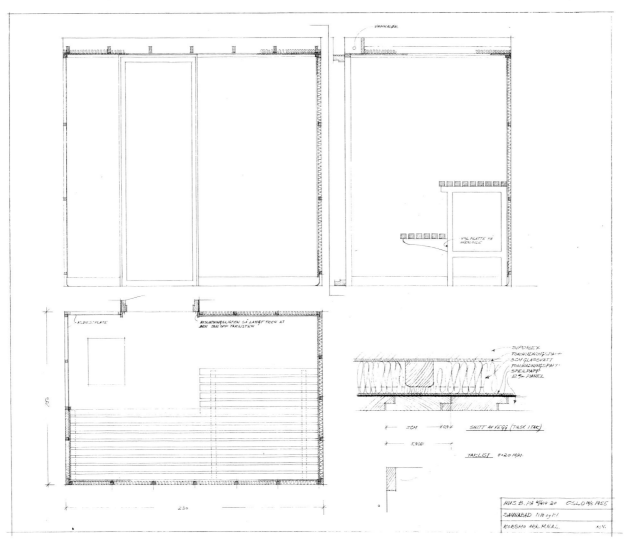

The sauna, 18 May 1955.

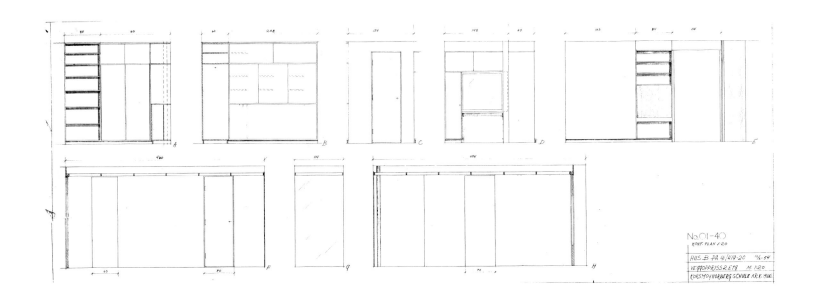

No.01-40
KONF. PLAN 1:20

HUS B PÅ 41/419-20   10/6-54
VEGGOPPRISS 2.ETG   M 1:20
KORSMO&NORBERG SCHULZ ARK.MNAL

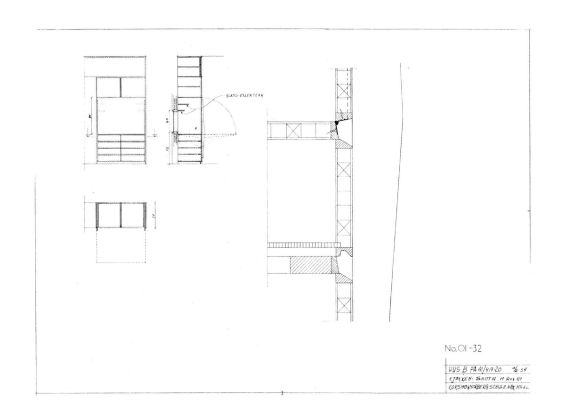

GLASS-ELLER TEAK

No.01-32

HUS B PÅ 41/419-20   10/6-54
KJØKKEN-SNITT M ROK 41
KORSMO&NORBERG SCHULZ ARK.MNAL

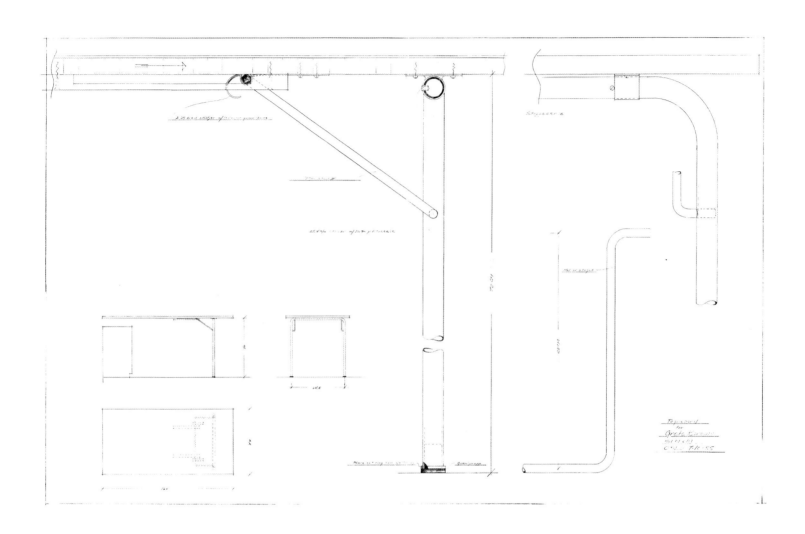

OPPOSITE TOP Interior elevations, upper floor, 10 May 1954.
OPPOSITE BOTTOM kitchen cabinets with window niche and
fold-down table top, 15 February 1954.
ABOVE Drawing table, 7 October 1955.

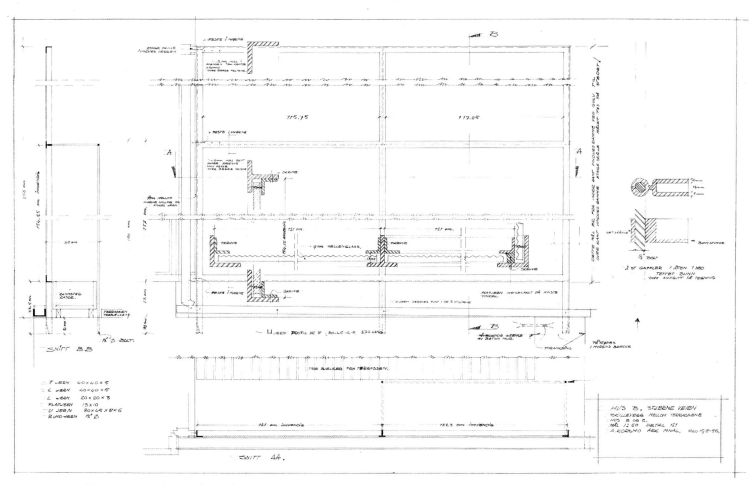

Combined screens/planters to partition the deck of no.12 from
those of the neighbouring houses, 15 August 1956.

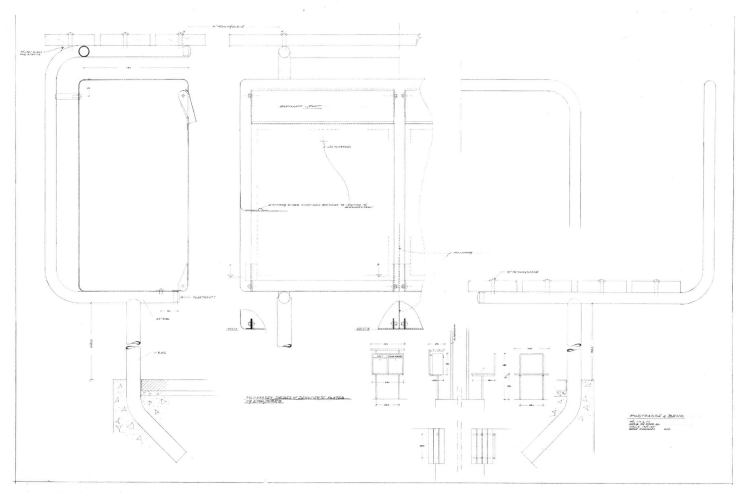

Mailbox and bench, 10 April 1955.

LEFT The houses seen from the west, 1955.
OPPOSITE A living room suffused with nature.

Once again we will travel back in time and immerse ourselves in the creation of the house in Planetveien and in the values that lie at its core. A literal translation of the title of Korsmo and Norberg-Schulz's article for *Byggekunst*, in which they presented the three attached houses, as "A threesome of dwellings by two of them". This is a reference to a classic Victorian travelogue, "Three in Norway (by Two of Them)",[128] which humorously describes the adventures of three British gentlemen in Norway. Written by two of the travellers, the book is illustrated with pen-and-ink sketches.

The friends' goal in the travelogue is to "fish our way up a string of lakes into the Jotunfjeld; getting there in time for the commencement of the reindeer hunting season."[129] The narrative contains many lyrical descriptions of nature, and as such had relevance to the three modern dwellings at the forest's edge. The book describes a rich, joyful and fruitful encounter between a foreign (in this case British) culture and life in the mountains of Norway. The travellers journey by horse and cart through Gudbrandsdalen and, despite the remoteness of their surroundings, manage to enjoy seven-course dinners in the finest Continental style. Any discomfort caused by the lack of the accoutrements of civilisation is compensated for by the joys of outdoor life. Korsmo and Norberg-Schulz chose the title as a kind of slogan, and it appeared in the printed article adjacent to a photograph depicting the fragile-seeming and precisely geometrical houses in the midst of untamed woods. The title also functioned as a device to conjure up a backdrop against which they could discuss the significance of nature for the architecture of the houses.

Openness and warmth

The architects introduced the article with some thoughts about openness, transparency and warmth (in the sense of "snugness"):

In Oslo we are fortunate that we still have a landscape in which we can delight, so let us enjoy it to the full so long as we are able. Of course, a precondition for making a house open towards its surroundings must be that there is something to look at. Accordingly it is by no means clear that the 'glass house' is an unnatural solution in Norway. We must merely ensure that we are able to create an appropriately intimate and snug atmosphere on a gloomy winter's evening. This was the straightforward idea behind the architectural approach for the attached houses on Vettakollen.[130]

In the case of Korsmo's house, the composition of the house as a whole, as well as its more detailed aspects, involves an orchestration of elements that both individually and together have the effect of combining "the transparent" and "the snug" into a symphonic composition. Beginning from the north with the living room, the dominant feature here is the sense of openness created by the sheer glass wall looking out towards the forest. This openness is softened, however, by the snug feeling created by the sunken nature of the space as a whole and of the area in front of the fireplace. The snug warm atmosphere is enhanced by the wall-to-wall carpeting, originally a warm-grey sisal, and the underfloor heating. Korsmo later regretted that he had not also had heating pipes installed within the tile-covered concrete wall where it ran below the

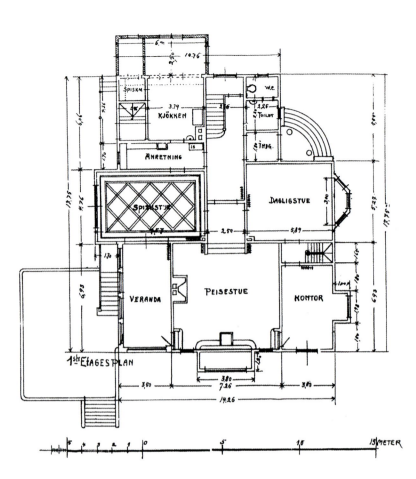

wall of windows.[131] The wall facing the street also has a quality of openness, although here it is moderated by the use of translucent, milk-white Thermolux panels. Only one panel, in the corner next to the fireplace wall, is transparent.

No.12 is the only house in the row in which the living room floor is excavated to lie below ground level. This result is a permanent variation that contrasts with the inherent flexibility of the attached houses' skeleton frames. Although there are many examples of the use of floor-level differentiation as an architectural device, one example in particular is worth mentioning here. Korsmo was "quite captivated" by the living room at "Solhaugen", the home of Grete's paternal grandparents, Hilda and

Toroit Prytz. The house, which was built around 1900, had been designed by Grete's grandfather.[132] The living room, which was similar in size to the living room at Planetveien, was also sunken from the rest of the ground floor and was accessed down three broad steps. Further similarities were that the living room at "Solhaugen" had a fireplace to one side, while windows along the whole front wall opened the room out towards the garden.

Another characteristic feature of Planetveien 12, which contributes to the feeling of warmth in the "hollow" formed by the living room, is the row of colourful cushions stacked against the low concrete wall along the wall of windows. This arrangement is quite different from, for example, the seating arrangements found in the Eames

House or the Farnsworth House. In both these houses, the seating furniture stands on the floor, and the floor "flows" outdoors on a single plane "through" the facade. However, some of Frank Lloyd Wright's houses, such as Fallingwater and Taliesin West, have sofas placed along very wide windows in a configuration that is reminiscent of the cushions at Planetveien. The Korsmos had visited both of these Wright houses. In addition, in Korsmo's house, the glass wall in the living room "flows" up and behind the edge of the suspended ceiling. This gives the space, whose sunken nature creates a strong sense of attachment to the ground, an opening upwards to treetops and the sky above.

The next zone, the hall, is transparent and translucent to an extreme degree. This is due to the glass doors set into the external walls at the front and back of the house and the glass roof above the translucent plastic panels that form the ceiling.

The third zone, the kitchen, is a snug, protected space that is the polar opposite of the transparent hall. The kitchen's teak walls are as "thick" as the cupboards

TOP: Fallingwater, sofas lining the wall of windows.
BOTTOM: Transparency and translucency in the hall.
RIGHT: Variations in snugness and openness.

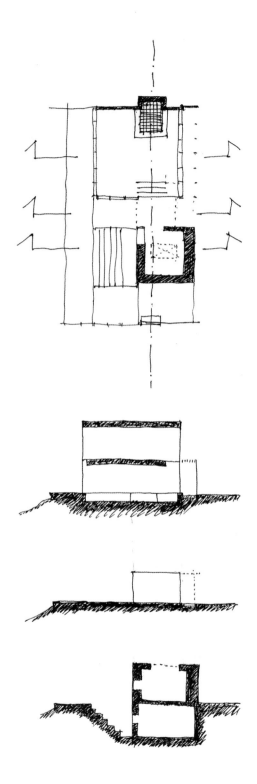

are deep and, apart from the translucent skylight in the centre of the ceiling, the room only has the one small window, which is set into one of the cupboards. Taking these three spaces together, it is possible to identify a "transparency/snugness" axis running from the fireplace, through the sunken but very open living room, on through the extremely transparent hall into the cave-like kitchen. By taking sections across the building at various points along this axis, we can see how this theme of "transparency vs. snugness" is also modulated in the vertical plane. This involves the use both of fragile skins of glass and deeply inset apertures in walls and roofs; and of sunken floor areas and the carefully considered excavation of areas next to the house.

Transparency and translucency

Three different materials are used to give the house its qualities of transparency and translucency. Firstly, there are the panes of clear window glass installed across large areas of wall. Secondly, there are the Thermolux panels used on the facade of the house, which while they transmit light, are too opaque to see through. Both these materials are used primarily in fields that fit into the framework of modules, each measuring 122 x 244 cm, that form a kind of rectangular filter or screen. Thirdly, the house features translucent plastic panels that are set into the ceilings underneath skylights. These panels also conceal electric light fittings, which can be used to supplement daylight or to replace it after dark. The orchestration of the transparent and translucent surfaces creates rich plays of light and reflections. In later life, Grete Prytz Kittelsen highlighted this as one of the most important features of life in the house.[133] On another occasion she described how the views of nature acted as a constant source of inspiration for her designs in silver and enamel.

> And the glass walls at home—when the light falls in here in all types of weather and is accompanied by the views of nature outside, that creates experiences of beauty, constant new effects that really fascinate me. [...] Winter is splendidly white, autumn is gold, there's

OPPOSITE TOP Sketch of ground floor plan
showing axis of snugness/openness.
OPPOSITE BOTTOM Sectional sketch showing
variations in snugness/openness.
TOP The Thermolux wall.
BOTTOM White rowan berries in front of
the Thermolux wall.

LEFT Reflections in the glass wall.
OPPOSITE Next to an upper floor window.

spring with 'mouse's ears [birch buds]' and the light, and the summer with beautiful flowers and greenery. As an enamel artist one has to learn to see. To see one's surroundings and to see what one is doing. To show sensitivity and analyse the task in hand.[134]

Thus the natural surroundings of the house are brought far inside it, with their proximity varying in vibrancy depending on the light from the sky, the vegetation outside and the wind and the weather. Their presence also acts to heighten one's experience of the dimension of time.

Various transparent, translucent and reflective materials are also used outdoors. One example is the lightweight structures of various heights that act as partitions from the neighbouring plots. As these structures descend the slope on either side of the plot, their design echoes the architecture of the house. Copies of the paintings made by Gunnar S Gundersen for one of the Triennale exhibitions are fixed to the partition that separates the plot from that of no.10, bringing art out into nature. When Grete Prytz Kittelsen celebrated her ninetieth birthday in the house, on 28 June 2007, those of us who were present could observe how the fire in the fireplace was reflected twice: first in the wall of windows, and then outdoors in the glass wall facing the neighbouring plot, so that a bonfire appeared to be burning far down the hillside.

Views of the landscape are visible from the house, framed differently depending on one's position. Originally the houses stood alone at the edge of the forest. Nowadays there are many more houses in the neighbourhood, although the border of the protected area of forest still runs across the end of Planetveien. Over the years the vegetation has grown, changing both the close-up and more distant views. A vigorous spruce tree stood for many years outside the living room of Planetveien 12. Viewed with great affection, it was known as "The Trolls in the Hedal Woods", because of its resemblance to the trolls in an illustrated version of the folk tale by Asbjørnsen and Moe.[135] The "trolls", which in time had become very large, were cut down a few years ago, when the new owners of no. 14

complained of lack of light. In any event, the concept was that the surrounding nature and the open qualities of the architecture would enrich the experience of dwelling, making it easy to move between the indoor and outdoor space. From this point of view, the attached houses in Planetveien were ahead of their time in their architectural use of glass in the Norwegian climate.

Japanese contemplativeness

Japanese architecture is often mentioned in the context of the attached houses in Planetveien. What affinities with Japanese buildings can we identify? The houses' design and construction bears no obvious direct relationship to the Japanese-style designs, characterised by exposed post-and-beam wood structures and large sliding doors, that we see in Danish houses, from the 1950s and 1960s. It is true that Korsmo had not (yet) been to Japan when the Planetveien houses were designed and built. Nevertheless, Japanese architecture had made a strong impression on him, ever since he saw in 1921 a Japanese tea room in the East Asia department of the Museum of Arts and Industry in Hamburg.

Korsmo pursued this interest during the war, in part through studying in the library in Stockholm. In addition, Korsmo and Jørn Utzon visited the tea house in the

OPPOSITE Light effects in the forest.
LEFT Light falling on the outdoor partition screens.
RIGHT View from the upper floor.

garden of the Ethnographic Museum at Djurgården in Stockholm on a spring day in 1945. This visit was to prove a significant experience for them both. Just over ten years later, Korsmo contributed an article to *Byggekunst*, titled "Japan and Western architecture", in which he discussed Japanese tea culture. He wrote that "People in the West need both nature and contemplation to relax—and we as architects encourage [the use of] and seek out materials for our spatial experiences precisely in order to achieve peace, quiet, tranquillity, and order."[136] Korsmo concluded the article with some remarks about the Japanese qualities of his new home at Planetveien 12:

> The fireplace satisfies, for example, the need to come to rest before the movement and sounds of fire. It gathers everyone who comes to the house in a ritual similar to that of the tea ceremony, a simple 'in-between' moment of heightened contemplative quiet—even though many are gathered together. If I had built the house as originally planned, with a

single large space and a sleeping area on a balcony only accessible by a ladder, I might have achieved a larger cube of air; the kind of bird cage shown in my original conceptual sketch. But it would not have provided me with the quiet and strength that precisely this balance gives between the closed and the open, between the kitchen, the hall and the living room, in the interplay between heights and materials.[137]

Japanese architecture thus forms a point of reference precisely for the emphasis on the interplay between snugness and transparency, as mentioned above, in Korsmo's house. He emphasises the importance of certain qualities of Japanese architecture, which he refers to as its "deepest secret", as also being of importance to modern Western architecture: lightweight construction methods, temporariness, and the flexible use of space. All three of these qualities, or principles, were crucial to the design of the house in Planetveien.

When teaching young architects, Korsmo often spoke enthusiastically about the tatami mat's "power to impose order", and about how repetition and variation in architectural composition could be conjured in innumerable versions from this one, simple element that was even based on the size of a person: approximately 3 x 6 feet. The tatami mat is used as a modular unit to create the spatial structure and configurations of Japanese houses—in the same way as a modular grid was used to determine the overall design of the attached houses in Planetveien. One might even say that the cushions in the Korsmos' living room were the equivalent of tatami mats, in that they were vehicles for repetition and variation, and that they were also a continuation of Japanese "floor culture"—the use of the floor as a place to sit during tea ceremonies and similar occasions.

Korsmo was particularly attracted by the fact that the original name for the room where the tea ceremony is held, sukiya, means both "house of the imagination" and "house of emptiness". The most striking characteristic of such a room is that it is totally free of ornament, with all utensils kept in closed cupboards. As a consequence, cupboards and shelves are permanently installed, as

TOP Translucent screens partition no.12 from the neighbouring garden.
BOTTOM Zui Ki Tei, the tea house in Stockholm.
OPPOSITE Gunnar S Gundersen paintings from the Milan Triennale on the partition against no.10.

is generally also the case in Korsmo's house. In his reflections on objects, space and architecture, Korsmo admired the Japanese for their restraint, the value ascribed to simplicity, and the moderation of their approach to everyday items. Korsmo pointed out that Japanese kitchen utensils and equipment were characterised by a simple, yet advanced, aesthetic value.[138] The "house of emptiness" is, in Korsmo's words, a house built for "a poetic impulse", a place that "remains unfinished so that one's imagination has something to complete".[139] As regards the importation of values of a more specifically architectonic nature from Japanese culture, Korsmo reminds the reader that Frank Lloyd Wright's efforts to introduce new abstract possibilities to architecture were based, according to Wright, not on studies of Japanese buildings, as has sometimes been suggested, but on studies of Japanese prints.[140]

Transforming sources of inspiration

Although the influence of Japanese architecture on the houses in Planetveien was complex and indirect, this does not make it any the less inextricably woven into the architectonic solutions and interiors. It is worth noting that in the same article Korsmo looks at how the process of creating architecture may be affected by direct and indirect sources of inspiration. According to Korsmo, although one may attempt to detect sources of inspiration, in this case Japanese sources, the sources of inspiration for an individual architect are so complex in their development that one should avoid any purely superficial aesthetic comparison. As Korsmo put it:

> For myself, even the experiencing of my own development and influences involves such a slow process of clarification that one should be extremely cautious. But it has struck me that I feel a very strong connection to the tranquillity and simplicity described by the author of the tea book.[141]

There is a striking compatibility between the aspects of Japanese architecture that were highlighted in architectural journals, and in Norwegian architecture teaching during the 1950s and 1960s, and the

ideology of Modernism. There was a shared interest in temporariness and flexibility, as well as in mass-production. These ideas were reflected in the photographs of Japanese interiors that were selected for publication and teaching purposes, which tended to depict sliding doors opening out to gardens, floors "flowing" from room to room, wooden posts, thin wooden lattice, and paper walls, all contrasted with beautiful rocks, mosses and pine tree branches outside. The ideal modernist house was a lightweight construction with horizontal beams and ceilings. This type of house fitted into a conceptual world characterised by rectangular, skeleton tectonics— and by rationality and a belief in progress.

The large, steep and heavy saddle roofs of traditional Japanese houses were generally ignored, however, apart from in an article by the Danish architect Nils-Ole Lund on Japanese farmhouses, which was accompanied by photographs and drawings of such roofs.[142] Rather,

OPPOSITE: The terraced garden seen from the workshop.
ABOVE: Looking down into the terraced garden in the lightwell.

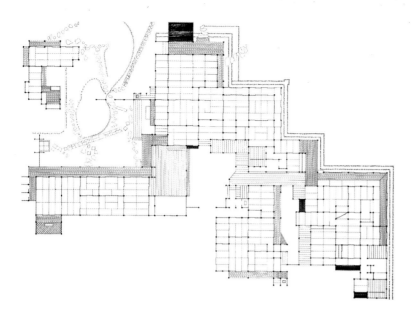

LEFT Katsura Imperial Villa, Kyoto, plan.
OPPOSITE LEFT "Creeping bellflower", from Emil Korsmo's *The Anatomy of Weeds*.
OPPOSITE TOP RIGHT Cross-section of a meadow buttercup from Emil Korsmo's *The Anatomy of Weeds*.
OPPOSITE BOTTOM RIGHT Material for a mountain school project.

as explained by the architect Gullik Kollandsrud in his article on Japanese architecture, "The homeland of the module", the concern was to identify inspiring parallels for approaching modern concerns such as flexible architecture, skeleton constructions and standardisation. Accompanying Kollandsrud's article, a plan of the Katsura Imperial Villa in Kyoto, depicting a domino-like arrangement of tatami mats, serves as a prime example of structuralist architecture with its additive structural principles applied to asymmetrical and, in theory, open and flexible, buildings.[143]

Structure and change

For Korsmo, the world of ideas and the experimental studies that he shared with Jørn Utzon were particularly important. Both the experiments at the National College of Applied Arts (SHKS) in Oslo and the testing of ideas relating to the realisation of the Planetveien project were at the forefront of what would later be characterised as Structuralism in Norwegian architecture. This involved designing buildings as complexes in accordance with a fixed system that allowed the use of a limited number of basic elements that could be repeated and varied in accordance with certain rules. It also involved creating and designing generally applicable solutions that would tolerate changes and variation. One principle, for example, is to separate load-bearing structures from non-load-bearing structures: by using a post-and-beam system for the main load-bearing structure, walls can be moved in order to partition or open space without affecting the basic structure of the building.

Jørn Utzon took Structuralism in the direction of a freer and more powerful geometrical "musicality" that surpassed the prevalent right-angled pragmatism. Utzon applied his approach to furniture systems, housing developments and university campuses, not to mention the building he was to become most famous for, the Sydney Opera House. Behind Utzon we can detect the influence of Aalto and, with regard to furniture, of both Eames and Saarinen. Analogies with biological structures, change and growth were central to Utzon's ideas, and stimulated the creation of a geometrical order that permitted the use of a broad repertoire of powerful structures and soft forms. For example, designs for load-bearing structures could be based on analogies to a plant's stalk, leaves and flowers with structural elements that were in principle identical, whether they were large or small, many or few.

As metaphorical support for the theories that Korsmo himself took as the basis for his views on structure, order

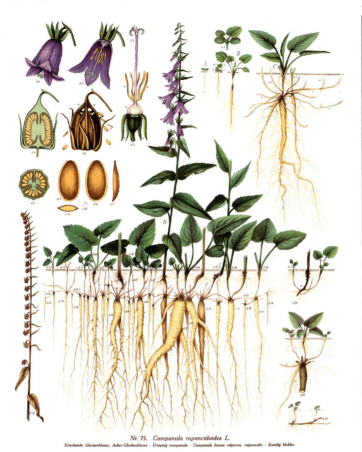

Nr. 75. *Campanula rapunculoides L.*
Kriechende Glockenblume, Acker-Glockenblume - Creeping campanula - Campanule fausse raiponce, raiponcette - Ettaldig klokke.

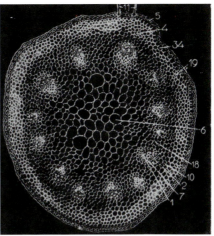

and freedom in architectural design, he often referred to the illustrations in his father's scientific volumes about the anatomy of weeds.[144] When Arne was a boy, his father told him: "So this is the plant from its root to its top. It has a Latin name that describes its qualities. You will see how it looks under the microscope. Its structure—the thing that makes it into a plant—is its architecture."[145]

Emil Korsmo, a pioneer of weed biology, was over 90 years old when he died in 1953. Before his death he had recently completed his multi-volume illustrated work *The Anatomy of Weeds*, which he had begun after retiring from his professorship at the Agricultural College of Norway (NLH). An enlargement of one of the botanical illustrations from this work was exhibited at the major Jørn Utzon retrospective held in 2004 at

the Louisiana Museum of Modern Art near Copenhagen, where Emil Korsmo was cited as one of the inspirations for Utzon's work. Although the tectonics—i.e. the general spatial design and structure—of the Planetveien house are rectangular, this type of "organic" thinking about structure and change resonates with the project as a whole.

As Terje Moe emphasised during one of our conversations, Korsmo was also capable of more playful designs, using flowering—almost Jugendstil—forms. As an example, Moe referred to a handle and a brass bannister that Korsmo had designed for the Britannia Hotel in Trondheim.[146] Korsmo also respected and admired the Belgian painter and architect Henry van de Velde, one of the founders of Art Nouveau, and often referred to his work.

10 • "HOME MECCANO"

A short article by Arne Korsmo in the PAGON edition of *Byggekunst* includes an explanation of the so-called "Home Meccano" method. The explanation is presented in the style of a plate with white text and images on a black background.[147] Both Korsmo himself and many of the people who have written about him have referred frequently to this explanation.

The term "Home Meccano" has proved to have considerable rhetorical force and, for the purposes of disseminating the concept, was a stroke of genius. Meccano was a model construction system that enjoyed enormous popularity among children in the 1950s. Produced by a toy manufacturer, Meccano kits (similar to what were known in the United States as Erector sets) consisted of aluminium strips in various standard lengths along with the nuts and bolts used to connect them. The metal strips had equidistant perforations and children could make all kinds of models and devices by bolting the strips together. Meccano was similar to the toy construction kits, consisting of perforated strips of beech connected by plastic nuts and bolts, launched in the 1970s by the Swedish toy manufacturer BRIO.

In his article about Home Meccano, Korsmo took as his starting point the economic difficulties encountered during post-war reconstruction. Although the economic situation necessitated a rationing of living space, Korsmo was critical of conventional houses, describing their discrete rooms as crammed together "like matchboxes". What was more, "Accordingly the rooms are becoming more and more cramped and less and less suitable for accommodating the conventional types of furniture that continue to be produced."[148]

For Korsmo, the damaging psychological effect—the "impulse of fear"—created by these small rooms became the motivating factor in his call for radical change. He called for scientific research into all aspects of dwelling and housing—not simply time-and-motion studies of housewives working in their kitchens. He proposed that such research should be undertaken by an "Institute of Usefulness", and specified that "shape, colour, i.e., design must be the subject of a more in-depth evaluation".[149]

The Home Meccano method takes up the ideas underlying Le Corbusier's early system houses developed during the First World War, in which the space could be configured freely by combining different units, each with a defined purpose. According to Korsmo, the purpose of such a system was psychological stimulation. The intention was to counteract passivity among the population and bring people's "desire for activity into motion so that they come to participate in the cultural environment—that whole which science assists in creating."[150] Korsmo's illustrated explanation of his Home Meccano method has an introductory paragraph that argues in favour of a working method and analysis of the individual, the home and the house—with the aim of giving the individual, the family and the environment the chance to free themselves from passivity and become consciously active in dwelling and building.[151]

As is the case in many of Korsmo's texts and lectures, his explanation of the Home Meccano method covers a very broad range of ideas. Adopting an associative approach, the text synthesises and embraces many different factors: human free will, human beings' use of the senses to orient themselves in space, principles governing growth in nature, and flexible living spaces. At the same time, Korsmo embarks on an analysis of structural elements that is informed by technical research and industrial development. He is committed to

Korsmo's plate explaining Home Meccano method.

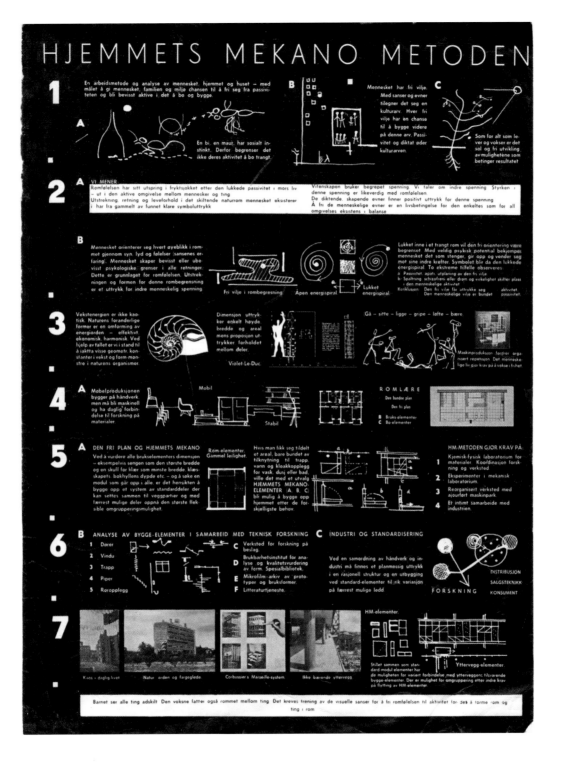

standardisation and points out that "the Japanese have mastered a flexible form of housing that we now with great difficulty must attempt to liberate ourselves sufficiently to adopt."[152]

For Korsmo, Home Meccano was the ability freely to configure standard units within the flexible living space. As Korsmo wrote, this would provide us with the greatest opportunity for self-expression using "the little with which we must be content". It would also enable us to achieve "rich variety with simple means".[153] Moreover: "The most essential aspect of Home Meccano is the experience of space, the variation in the actual rooms and not the actual objects. [...] In the wholeness of the interaction lies the opportunity for the greatest meeting of energy and therefore the highest expression of life."[154]

Typically for Korsmo, the language of the article is both dramatic and inspirational. Inspirational perhaps most of all because it spans such a breadth of ideas and can be interpreted in so many different ways. Occasionally the logic becomes slightly disconnected and it becomes impossible to pinpoint his meaning precisely. This quality in itself embodies a sense of openness and movement.

ABOVE 48 m² apartment, National College of Applied Arts, Oslo.

The function of the built-in cupboards

The Italian architect Gennaro Postiglione has described Home Meccano as "an analytic method that places the design of the various constituent parts of the house, including the furnishing, in direct relation, using a square grid as the module of reference".[155] It is true that certain elements of the interior of Planetveien 12 relate to the module used to determine the overall design of the house, in that the walls of cupboards are sometimes—but far from always—designed with dimensions that are compatible with this module. Even so, Postiglione's explanation does not clarify what Home Meccano actually involves when it is applied as a system or method. It is certainly true that the overall layout of the three houses in Planetveien is based on a modular grid, and it is also true that the dimensions of the 100 square cushions and of the wall of cupboards in the living room of no.12 are compatible with the same module. Apart from those features, however, the interior elements in the house are neither particularly standardised nor based on that module's dimensions. In fact, the opposite is the case, with the individual elements being both custom-designed and permanently installed, with their various individual modules or subdivisions unified visually by their uniform, smooth surfaces that are devoid of mouldings or other ornament.

As already mentioned, the walls of cupboards function either as floor-to-ceiling partitions, or as a kind of thick cladding or "lining" inside the external walls. As in the case of the 80 m² experimental apartment constructed at the National College of Applied Arts (SHKS) in Oslo, the objective was to fit "as much as possible into the walls of cupboards".[156] And, as was the case in the 48 m² apartment, "the walls are clad with cupboards".[157] Table tops and beds can be folded out of the cupboards, shutters made of wooden slats can be used to screen off the kitchen worktop, while the use of heavier and more static pieces of furniture—such as free-standing beds, sofas and wardrobes—is avoided completely.[158] The unified approach to materials and workmanship is emphasised by discrete details: the "piano hinges" used for the hinged doors, and the Japanese-style triple finger pulls on the sliding doors. These various interior elements form part of the defining characteristics of the space, rather than functioning as conventional free-standing furniture or space-limiting partitions.

Even though the construction of a building may be module-based, there is no requirement that this module must determine the design of its interior. Principles underlying the design of cupboards may perfectly well be unrelated to any module that determined a dwelling's layout and structural design. This was the case in the Korsmos' previous apartment in Løchenveien, where the interior elements were installed in a pre-existing house. On the other hand, the use of custom-designed built-in furniture as an important element in the architecture of a space is a tradition followed by the Belgian architect Henry van de Velde, Frank Lloyd Wright and Le Corbusier, as well as the Austrian architect Adolf Loos and the Dutch architect Gerrit Rietveld. Another closely related example is the use by the Austrian-American architect Rudolph M Schindler of walls of plywood cupboards as non-loadbearing partitions in his low-cost, mass-producible "Schindler Shelters", developed during the 1930s.[159]

From this perspective, the built-in cupboards in Planetveien, with their inherent flexibility as regards use, can be seen as a deliberate device to create order and cater for a range of functions. The objective was to increase the available floor space and generally to create a sense of open space. The Norwegian word for an item of furniture "møbel" derives from the Latin mobilis, meaning mobile or moving. In Korsmo's interior, mobility is used deliberately: conventional, specialised and heavy furniture is discarded in favour of lightweight, manageable basic items, such as cushions and lightweight wicker tables with removable trays.

PLANETV. 7008

OPPOSITE Kitchen cabinet doors and the piano hinge
on the door in the kitchen.
RIGHT Proposal for further housing development
along Planetveien, 1 March 1955.

Home Meccano as a principle for housing development

The architects Finn Kolstad and Terje Moe, who both worked closely with Korsmo while he was teaching in Trondheim, interpret the Home Meccano method in relation to the project in Planetveien as a design principle for housing development. According to this interpretation, the application of the method would allow an area to be developed with houses that, despite their differing spatial solutions and differing facades, would all be designed in accordance with the same principle, namely, in this case, a module measuring 122 cm horizontally and 244 cm vertically. This module would govern the dimensions of the houses' alternating one- and two-storey units, with all facades consisting of rectangular fields of either white-painted fibre cement panels or glass.[160] This brings us back to the use of a module to determine a building's overall design. Kolstad and Moe's interpretation accords with the structuralist principles that underlay Korsmo's earlier experiments at the National College of Applied Arts, as well as ideas current within CIAM and architectural circles internationally at that time. Korsmo also prepared a proposal to build an additional 12 similar houses further up towards the forest on Vettakollen, mostly on the other side of Planetveien.[161] The architect Bjørn Wærenskjold remembers that Korsmo gave his students in Trondheim an assignment to design one of these houses, intended for Gunnar S Gundersen, on a plot opposite nos. 10–14.[162] In the event, these houses were never built.

The rhetorical force of the expression "Home Meccano method" lies perhaps precisely in the fact that it should not be taken too literally. It is not a rigid method of either analysis or construction. Rather, it is an expression of a way of thinking, of a general approach to the organisation of buildings, spaces and interiors. From this point of view, standardisation is just one of several factors to be taken into account.

Meccano and mechanical engineering symbolise matter, power, energy and movement. Korsmo succeeds in adapting this powerful metaphor to appeal to people's—and not least children's—free, playful power. In his explanation of the method, he adds motivating expressions such as, for example, "energy spiral" and links his ideas to the engineering- and science-based buildings he expects in the future. By linking "Meccano" to the word "home", he is also able to connect with the strong emphasis placed in the post-war period on family, family life and home-building. The rhetorical power of Home Meccano lies in this striking synthesis.

LEFT The cupboards with reversible doors above
the fireplace.
TOP The ceiling with loudspeakers and light fittings
to illuminate the blackboards.
BOTTOM Detail of the stairs.
OPPOSITE Korsmo's Christmas blackboard drawing
on a cupboard door.

11 • MODULES WITH VARIATIONS

Leaving aside the general enthusiasm within Modernism for steel structures, the closest sources of inspiration for the use of steel in the Planetveien project were Charles Eames and Ludwig Mies van der Rohe. Arne Korsmo knew both men, and Christian Norberg-Schulz was a great admirer of Mies.

Throughout his life, one of Norberg-Schulz's favourite expressions was "a clear structure" and he considered Mies to be the "godfather" of the Planetveien project.[163] In this he was not referring in particular to the actual use of steel in the houses' structure, but to the primary architectonic importance allocated to the steel structure and its importance for refining the architectural design. For his part, Arne Korsmo referred more frequently to Eames than to Mies. Eames' work and working methods were probably more in tune with Korsmo's temperament, as Korsmo's approach was more complex, rich and unpredictable. For Korsmo, perfection had more to do with the poetry of composition than doctrinaire adherence to architectural principles.

Elements and experiments

Industrialisation, and the ideas it provoked about mass-producible housing and modular design, were fundamental to Modernism. Rudolph M Schindler's "shelters" were an early example of this type of housing. The shelters were small, mass-producible single-storey detached dwellings. Designed for labourers, the first shelters were based on a five-foot module and were built in 1934 using Neal Garrett's patented hollow concrete slabs. As early as 1935, however, Schindler abandoned Garrett's slabs in favour of a four-foot module that used a wooden framework with plywood panels. In Schindler's opinion, the smaller module was more appropriate for a small dwelling.

Schindler had used a four-foot module previously, in 1920. In his view, layouts created using a four-foot module, along with subdivisions of that module (halves, thirds and quarters), were more flexible. In addition, as well as harmonising better with human proportions, it was also more convenient given the building materials that were available in California at that time.[164] In 2006, the American architectural historian Jorge Otero-Pailos suggested that the "Schindler shelters" might have been the inspiration for the row of three attached houses in Planetveien.[165] In fact, however, the only common feature is the use of a four-foot module: the buildings' architecture and construction, as well as the actual uses to which the module is put, are very different.

Otero-Pailos also proposed Schindler's own house, built in 1922 in King's Road in Los Angeles, as a possible inspiration for the project in Planetveien. Although it is most unlikely that the Korsmos visited the Schindler house while they were in Los Angeles, and never explicitly referred to it as an inspiration for their own dwelling, the King's Road project does share certain features with Planetveien 12. Both Schindler and Korsmo designed their houses as spaces where a couple could both live and work; both houses have unconventional layouts; and ideas about prefabrication—in Schindler's case using load-bearing concrete elements— were important to the design of both houses. In addition, both houses feature other architectonic devices—the use of wood and glass, and the feeling of closeness to nature— that are reminiscent of two objects of Korsmo's admiration: Japanese architecture, and the architecture of Frank Lloyd Wright. When describing the houses in Planetveien, Korsmo wrote:

> The two-storey section of each house has a steel skeleton as the load-bearing structure. The purpose of this skeleton is to allow more freedom with the layout

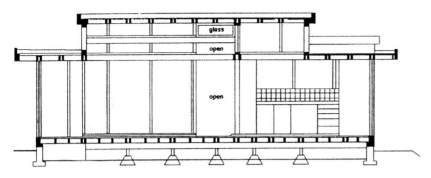

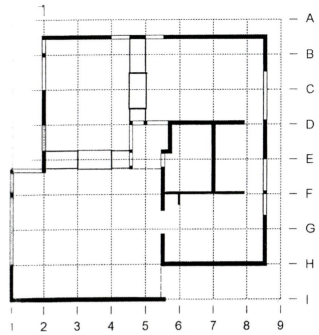

ABOVE AND TOP RIGHT: Schindler Shelters, an example.
BOTTOM RIGHT: King's Road House, Los Angeles, USA.

and to give us the opportunity to install glazing where required. The same type of skeleton is used in all the houses in order to allow the building components to be standardised. A wooden framework is bolted onto the outside of the skeleton. This framework serves as a support for glazing or insulating wall sections. These walls have an outer cladding of flat Eternit [fibre cement] panels. The cubic four-foot module was selected on the basis of the standard dimensions of the building materials.

The skeleton was dimensioned such that the load-bearing columns had a cross-section of only 8 x 8 cm where there was a span of 12 [or 24] feet.[167]

The use of standardised components was thus an important consideration for, and aspirational goal of, the project. In reality, however, the only standardised components used were the fibre cement panels used in the facade. Construction panels of various types were supplied in standard sizes, including 4 x 8 foot (building materials were not yet generally available in metric dimensions). "Thermopane" panels were in use at that time, but were unusual. If one considers the use of building materials in the interiors of the house, few elements accord with the four-foot module apart from the windows and Thermolux panels/sections, which were no doubt specifically ordered for the project.

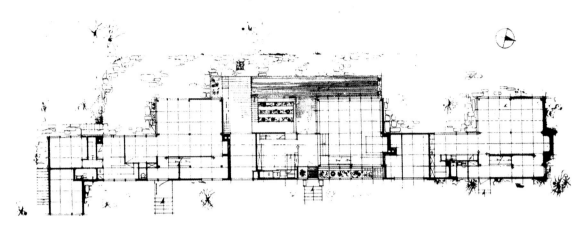

Plan, første etasje, mål 1 : 400.

Module and structure—conformity and non-conformity

In his *Byggekunst* article, Otero-Pailos highlights a lack of structural consistency in the Planetveien houses. A close study of the architects' drawings and of the houses as realised reveals that, in the two-storey sections of the houses, the 122 x 122 cm (4 foot) modular grid governs the layout inside the external walls. In the case of no.12, this area of the external walls is glazed, with a centre-to-centre distance between each wooden mullion of 122 cm. The same applies to the south-facing wall around the corner, i.e., the wall adjoining the exit to the terrace. However, the module "did not fit" in the section of facade where the entry door is located, i.e., the section between the living room and the kitchen. This part of the facade, which originally consisted of a pair of hinged doors (now replaced by a sliding door), was made narrower in order to accommodate the thickness of the glass wall where it rounds the corner.

Conceptually, the module was central to the project, and there is no doubt that a modular system is excellent when drawing at a small scale. The realities of wall thicknesses and other factors, however, may quickly thwart the application of the conceptual ideal. For this reason, a consistently executed modular design will often use load-bearing structural elements that are symmetrical, for example, with a square or cruciform cross-section, and that are centred over the grid. This type of dilemma must have arisen during the design of the three houses. The result was that the centre-to-centre distance, or module, between the load-bearing steel columns is smaller, at 354 cm, than the 3 x 4 foot (3 x 122 cm = 366 cm) module that governs the design of the facade. This apparent discrepancy is necessary to accommodate the thickness of the steel columns themselves as well as to allow an 8 cm airspace between the steel columns and the wooden framework of the external walls. This airspace is important not least to achieve the desired sense of spatial freedom that is created by the seeming lack of any connection between the steel structure that supports the upper floor and roof, and the external walls that support only themselves.

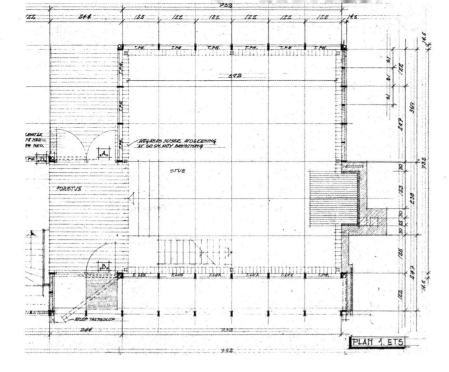

A "raincoat" on the outside

Otero-Pailos is correct in observing that early proposals for the project envisaged the steel skeleton as standing outside the external walls. Grete Prytz Kittelsen also explained that in the initial sketches, not only were the columns on the outside but the steel beams were above the roof, so that the whole house "hung like a bag" inside the steel structure.[169] This solution would have highlighted the steel skeleton in a way reminiscent of the architecture of Mies van der Rohe, as exemplified in buildings such as his Farnsworth House, close to the Fox River, Illinois, and his buildings for the Illinois Institute of Technology in Chicago.

It is uncertain whether it was Korsmo or Norberg-Schulz who pushed through the final choice of an internal steel skeleton. But as Terje Moe has said: "It would have been pointless to have had the steel structure on the outside in Norway—the sensible solution was to have the "raincoat" on the outside and then everything else that wasn't rain resistant inside".[170] In Ray and Charles Eames' house in California the steel columns are an integral part of the wall. This would appear to be the logical and straightforward solution, but in the Norwegian climate the resulting thermal bridge would have caused insurmountable problems.[171]

Otero-Pailos is mistaken, however, when he claims that the steel structure is unnecessary and that the wooden framework of the facade could have supported the house, i.e., the floor and roof of the upper floor. The whole facade, the wooden framework for the glass and fibre cement panels, is designed to form an equal frame around the infill elements. In other words, the horizontal wooden elements or transoms lie flat (like shelves) so that—like the mullions—they have the appearance of narrow glazing bars. As a result the whole building envelope appears lightweight and freestanding. If the wooden structure had fulfilled the primary load-bearing function, the transoms would have had to be of much greater dimensions. In that case, the mullions would have also been required to be of corresponding strength. In addition, the span of 732 cm between the external walls in no.12 would have been too great to be supported by a conventional load-bearing wooden structure. When

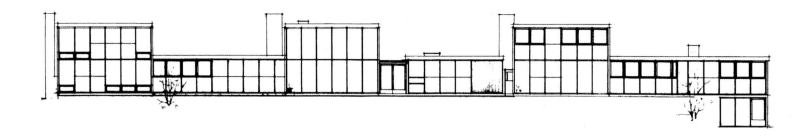

addressing claims that the houses in Planetveien are in fact examples of traditional wooden architecture, it is worth noting that the detailed drawings for the joinery work specify not only mortise-and-tenon joints, but also high-quality materials that are more associated with cabinet-making than with traditional Norwegian house-building.

A hybrid structure

The whole structure of the building is a hybrid. While the unobstructed space created by the slender steel skeleton provides the desired sense of spatial freedom in the main two-storey volumes, the wooden structure used in the single-storey sections, with its load-bearing studwork and roof joists, provides adequate room for manoeuvre. The emphasis on the 4 foot module as the basic determining factor for the design and ornament of the building is essential to its overall appearance, and is underscored by the fact that only every other stud in the single-storey section—the distance between these studs corresponding to the breadth of a fibre cement panel—is apparent on the facade.

The houses in Planetveien are often described as steel-and-glass houses. While this is only partially true, it nonetheless aptly sums up the architects' preoccupation with steel construction and the move at the time towards new types of construction in architecture in general. The first drawings and descriptions of possible steel structures for the three houses are dated as early as May 1952, and the architects continued to revise the concept during the design process. For a long time the drawings show a steel structure that continues through the whole row of

houses with columns spaced three modules, i.e., 12 foot (366 cm), apart, even in the single-storey sections. In the case of Korsmo's house, this would have meant having a steel column in the middle of the kitchen. As finally realised, this section of the house is instead constructed with wooden studwork. The 2" x 8" rafters, spaced at a distance of 61 cm centre-to-centre, span a distance of 488 cm between the external walls.[172]

In Planetveien 12, Korsmo adapted this hybrid construction system further by removing the steel column that, according to the 354 cm modular grid for the steel structure, should have stood in the middle of the living room. This alteration caused an imbalance in the loading of the building, necessitating a drastic increase in the specifications for the overhead steel beams, from I-16 to I-30. Although Korsmo had studied civil engineering at NTH before transferring to the architecture course, the actual structure of the building was for him more of a means to achieve a satisfactory spatial solution than an end in itself.

The discussion in Otero-Pailos' article about Norberg-Schulz's ideas on the theoretical importance of the square and, more specifically, the problems surrounding the central column in Planetveien 14, is interesting. In relation to the Planetveien houses, however, a more pragmatic interpretation may be just as relevant. Apart from not wanting to incur extra costs by removing the central column in the living area of no.14, Norberg-Schulz was also more of a purist in his approach to architecture than Korsmo. Given that the decision had been made to use a modular system, the young Norberg-Schulz would probably have considered that it should be adhered to, even cherished. Korsmo, by contrast, would have prioritised the spatial design as a whole, rather than allowing himself to be governed by the modular system and related principles. It is also striking how Norberg-Schulz accentuated the steel skeleton of his own house, no.14, by painting the steel red (incidentally, using the same colour as that used in Craig Ellwood's Case Study House #16), and painting the internal wooden framework the same white colour as the walls. Meanwhile, in no.12, Korsmo toned down the impact of the steel columns by painting them a greyish-white and used the ceiling to conceal the steel beams above it.

A forerunner of Structuralism

In spite of Korsmo's architectonic downplaying of the structural elements of his house, there seems to be no doubt that the houses in Planetveien are strong exponents, or at least significant forerunners, of Structuralism, a movement that was to flourish in Norwegian architecture in the 1960s and 1970s. The preoccupations of Structuralism, with its emphasis on the modular grid and "open structures" shown in the early drawings, are in the end most clearly expressed in the facades of the houses, composed as they are within a rhythmical rectangular grid of Oregon pine filled respectively with opaque, translucent and transparent panels.

In the interior of no.12, this modular grid, which is most conspicuous in the walls of windows, is just one of several elements that combine to create the overall designed environment. Perhaps Korsmo's nuanced application of the principles of modular design and his sophisticated handling of other spatial devices within the constraints of the modular system demonstrate precisely an enriching breadth of variations—and a liberating potential—for architectural design in general.

OPPOSITE West elevation of the row of attached houses.
RIGHT Sections showing steel and timber structures.

12 • A POETIC FRAMEWORK FOR DWELLING

Different ideas, designs and solutions may arise in parallel in different places, quite independently of each other. Similarly, people whose work is creative may be preoccupied with similar concerns at the same time, even if they do not have direct contact. This is true in the arts, as well as in science, technology and culture in a wider sense.[173] Arne Korsmo's exceptional sensibility and his endlessly enquiring mind made him an important player in this broad cultural context.[174]

Architectural design
—an associative creative process

The list of potential sources that may have influenced Korsmo's house in Planetveien is long, and may be interpreted in many different ways. How these interpretations are expressed will also depend on the interpreter's point of view—and on the context within which they arise. Here we are at the core of what may easily be overlooked if one is preoccupied merely with comparing projects and buildings as they are presented, without being aware of the associative and creative process of the architectural design. It is however absolutely essential to acknowledge that the designer at all times is accumulating and developing an apparent chaos of creative impulses from all directions; and that fragments and traces from different contexts may turn up in an upheaval with others, and then be transformed and refined in the creation of specific new works. Some of the wide-ranging associations that seem relevant for Planetveien 12 are mentioned below.

Gennaro Postiglione has suggested a connection between Korsmo's house in Planetveien and old Norwegian log houses, although this view has not garnered support among Norwegian architects.[175] This comparison may have an element of truth in relation to space and its furnishing and use, in that many different activities take place in the same room—as in the Hjeltarstua log house in the open-air museum at Maihaugen. This house has a square living area that is almost as large as the living room in Korsmo's house and similarly has the furniture placed along the walls. A non-Norwegian architect may also be struck by remarkable similarities in the architectonic simplicity of the buildings—their informality and lack of monumentality—that is characteristic both of the Planetveien houses and traditional Norwegian buildings in general. Like their modernist colleagues the world over, Norwegian architects were also eager to break with traditional forms, especially those most associated with bourgeois values. Korsmo however included the study of traditional Norwegian rural buildings in his teaching of young architecture students. These buildings were not studied as examples of features to avoid, but as important places to visit and learn from.

In her discussion of Korsmo's house in Planetveien, the art historian Astrid Skjerven has shown the influence of the French architect Pierre Chareau's Maison de Verre in Paris, built in 1928.[176] The construction of the two buildings is separated by nearly 30 years (and a World War), but they do have some features in common. Among other characteristics, they share a varied and sophisticated use of steel and glass, and the use of several new and unusual materials. The similarity between the internal staircase in Planetveien 12 and the retractable steel staircase in Chareau's house is obvious. The atmosphere within the two houses may also be said

At dusk.

TOP LEFT Aldo van Eyck, Municipal Orphanage, Amsterdam.
TOP RIGHT Different treatments of columns in Villa Mairea, Finland.
BOTTOM Aulis Blomstedt, attached houses in Tapiola, Finland.

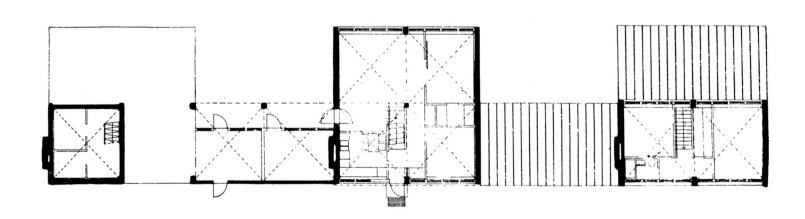

to have some similarities. The French architect wished to promote standardisation, but even so his house is "tailor-made" to an unusual extent, and is significantly more complex and luxurious than the Norwegian house.[177]

Obvious sources of inspiration for Planetveien, such as the architects Charles Eames, Ludwig Mies van der Rohe and Frank Lloyd Wright have already been mentioned. Another is the Dutch architect Aldo van Eyck. Korsmo knew van Eyck from his international contacts through CIAM, and was particularly impressed by van Eyck's famous Municipal Orphanage in Amsterdam. This was designed more or less at the same time as Planetveien, and with its square modular grid offered an example of a transformable architecture: an architecture that encourages the possibilities that arise from "open design" and that at the same time secures both the basic needs of human beings and their spiritual growth.[178]

Among the Nordic architects who deserve a place in Korsmo's "sphere of influence" is the Finnish architect Alvar Aalto and his unique Villa Mairea, which the Korsmos visited several times. Although this building is very different from the house in Planetveien, not least in its complexity and size, both houses are rich and varied in their spatial design. The individual parts of the Villa Mairea are carefully designed and detailed without detracting from the overall effect, which on the contrary integrates all these individual elements. For example, the freestanding load-bearing columns inside the external walls at Villa Mairea are, like the steel columns in Korsmo's house, treated as an element of the spatial design of the room, rather than being highlighted as part of a general structural system. In particular, the columns at Villa Mairea are painted in different colours and in some cases are also clad with wooden slats or wrapped in rattan. The blue ceramic tiles on the external wall against the neighbouring house in Planetveien are also reminiscent of the exterior of the Finnish house. Villa Mairea is however significantly larger and far more luxurious. The floor area of the square living area is approximately four times larger than that of the living room at Planetveien 12.

The houses in Planetveien also have certain features in common with the attached houses designed by the Finnish architect Aulis Blomstedt and built in 1954 in Tapiola, outside Helsinki. These houses, which have a module-based design, consist of double-height main volumes linked by smaller shallow single-storey sections. The dimensions of the buildings are approximately the same as those of the houses in Planetveien. According to the Danish architect Professor Nils-Ole Lund, Blomstedt's status among architects in Finland was similar to that enjoyed by Korsmo in Norwegian architectural circles. Blomstedt was professor of architecture from 1958 until 1966. He was also an influential architectural thinker, whose approach was characterised by "the same singular combination of a quest for order and the cultivation of cosmic phenomena" as was maintained by Korsmo.[179] Korsmo often referred to Blomstedt's attached houses in his lectures to Norwegian architecture students.

Planetveien 12 as *Gesamtkunstverk*

In Planetveien 12, the neutral and flexible architectonic structure of the house—which accords with the aims of Home Meccano—becomes the starting point for a confidently balanced almost classical composition of spaces with different characteristics. Not least the square "hollow" of the living room contributes to this feeling of balance, which in turn is softened by asymmetry, variation and the substantial degree of openness in the overall spatial composition of the house. In addition to Structuralism, Planetveien 12 seems to prefigure other architectural trends that would become important in the decades leading up to the turn of the twenty-first century and up until today. During that period, many architects abandoned architectonic principles requiring a clear visual relationship between a building's structure and its spatial design in favour of more pragmatic approaches. As a result the load-bearing structure could be "wrapped up" and concealed by surfaces used to "design" the space.

One could object that the sense of "balance" in Planetveien 12 has been achieved at the expense of flexibility, that is, the ability to make changes and

BELOW Objects made of silver and enamel by Grete Prytz Kittelsen.
OPPOSITE Both snug and open.

alterations. It is worth noting, however, how highly valued—over a period of more than 50 years—the house has been as a dwelling and workplace. And also how adaptable the house has proved to be to changing circumstances, including accommodating the needs of the house's ageing inhabitants, as exemplified by the simple changes that Prytz Kittelsen and her second husband made to the interior. Even after her husband died in 2002, Prytz Kittelsen continued to live in the house alone.

Planetveien 12 proved to be a good place simply to be, whether for many or just a few persons. The house simultaneously invites one to partake both of its intimate atmosphere and of magnificent spatial experiences. The house's qualities and general appeal are accordingly not insignificant. Even so, the house's inhabitants have had to collaborate with the architecture when making changes to the interior, as certain important premises are pre-determined. One change to the interior consisted of the addition of a few items of seating furniture and bookshelves. In addition, over the years, more of the 100 cushions have come to be covered in red fabric. Previously blue and grey were more predominant. In addition the cushions were stacked higher, so that they were more convenient as seating for older people.

Planetveien 12 may in fact be considered as a form of *Gesamtkunstwerk*, where objects, art, the interior and the architecture all combine to form a thoroughly conceived, complete and integrated composition.[180] Every element, both large and small, has been carefully selected and designed to fit into the larger whole. The Korsmos and their friends and collaborators had a wide range of skills and talents—from silversmithing, furniture design and fine art to architecture and urban planning. Not least, the contribution of the painter Gunnar S Gundersen was of decisive significance. The fact that Korsmo himself did not use the term *Gesamtkunstwerk* to describe Planetveien 12 may be explained by the fact that he did not wish to be associated with the Arts and Crafts Movement, as the term was widely used within that movement and often associated with its ideas.

Korsmo identified to a greater extent with the cross-disciplinary milieu of designers, artists and architects who were fascinated by the ideas of the Bauhaus school, which existed first in Weimar, then in Dessau (from 1925 to 1932) and finally in Berlin (from 1932). The Bauhaus, which was headed by Walter Gropius from 1919, was based on a close collaboration between engineers, architects and fine artists, as well as representatives from other creative fields. The school itself was an experiment,

a place for conducting research into modern technology and aesthetics. Mies van der Rohe was the rector of the school from 1930 until this important educational institution was dissolved in 1933. Later the architects of the Bauhaus were extremely influential both elsewhere in Europe and in the United States.

Korsmo, like so many other architects, drew inspiration from many sources, but made the different concepts and ideas "his own", adapting them and applying them on

his own terms. Korsmo frequently referred to the concept of *Raumkunst* ("the Art of Spatial Design"). This concept, while certainly related to that of *Gesamkunstwerk*, is used more specifically in the context of architecture and related disciplines. In addition to the aesthetics, *Raumkunst* covers all the technical and user-related aspects of architecture. On one occasion when Korsmo was asked in what field he worked, he answered:

"*Raumkunst!* That is a concept we haven't yet developed here in Norway. It is the art of coordinating the overall concept with dimensions on all levels, with rhythm, colour and form, and that becomes music."

To the follow-up question, "So what is architecture?", Korsmo replied:

"Architecture is the great ordering factor in the arts. It is the least free, tied as it is to the place, to money and to materials."[181]

An outstanding example of spatial design

The nature of the concepts of *Gesamkunstwerk* and *Raumkunst* had to be adapted to meet demands for change and flexibility; ideas that became so important in the 1950s and 1960s. In cases where these concepts have to encompass "user participation"—the idea that the building's inhabitants will also contribute to the architectonic solution, as Korsmo advocated in his Home Meccano method, the architect's role changes, and his field of operations is expanded. Often an architect will go a long way towards determining the interior design and the choice of objects that he or she considers important to the spatial environment, but there are some decisions that ultimately must be left to the inhabitants of the house. In the case of Planetveien 12, both the original inhabitants were involved in the design. In the years when Prytz Kittelsen continued to live in the house with her second husband, they made alterations to adapt the house to their changing requirements, but also ensured that the house's most important qualities were preserved.

Grete Prytz Kittelsen died in the autumn of 2010. Shortly afterwards, the Cultural Heritage Management Office in Oslo proposed that the exteriors of the three attached houses in Planetveien should be preserved. In addition, a process was commenced to secure a protection order to preserve the whole of no.12, including the built-in furnishings and a selection of furniture and objects that have special significance (such as the 100 cushions). As of May 2013, this process was nearing a conclusion, although the order had not yet been issued. ICOMOS Norway, a few other institutions and some private individuals had suggested that Planetveien 12 should become a kind of museum, which could be open to the public by appointment. Grete Prytz Kittelsen herself, however, wanted the house to continue to serve as a private residence. She disliked the idea of it becoming a lifeless museum object.[182] It should continue to be an everyday dwelling, she thought, a house to live in.

Planetveien 12 was sold in the spring of 2011. The buyers, a young couple with children, moved in shortly thereafter and undertook some repairs and improvements in close collaboration with Oslo's cultural heritage authorities. Although we know little about the future use of the row of attached houses, it is clear that Planetveien 12 and its immediate surroundings are guaranteed a certain amount of protection. And that Arne Korsmo and Grete Prytz Kittelsen's unique house will always have a special and important place in the history of Norwegian architecture. The house's architectural idiom belongs to a different era. But as an example of good and functional architecture it may continue to inspire designers and architects in Norway, as well as visitors from elsewhere with an interest in architecture.

Perhaps it is the house's sustained quality of compositional balance—the consciously designed environment created by the use of glass and a selection of other well-chosen materials and colours—that makes it an example of world-class architecture. Here one may experience the value of an excellent sense of design and study more closely some of the ideals and principles that were, and were to become, ground-breaking in modern architecture. The architecture of Planetveien is both simple and rich, both functional and flexible. The house provides a frame that is unassuming, yet at the same time poetic, for the act of living.

SURVEY DRAWINGS

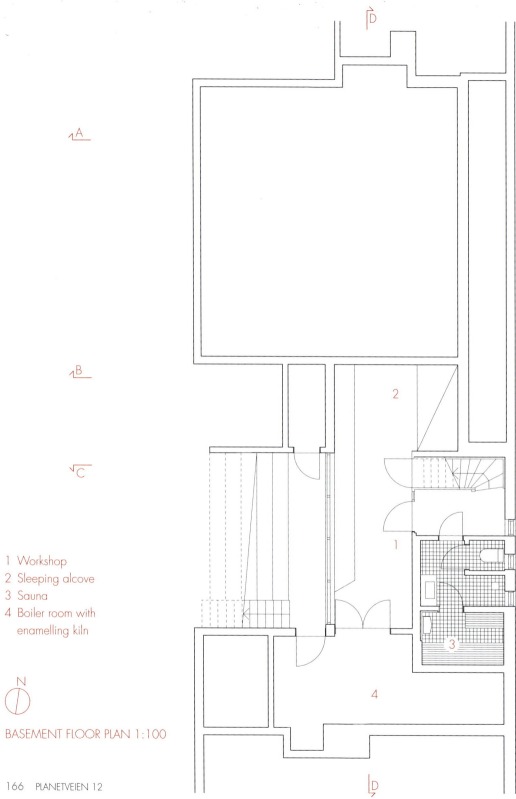

1 Workshop
2 Sleeping alcove
3 Sauna
4 Boiler room with
  enamelling kiln

N

BASEMENT FLOOR PLAN 1:100

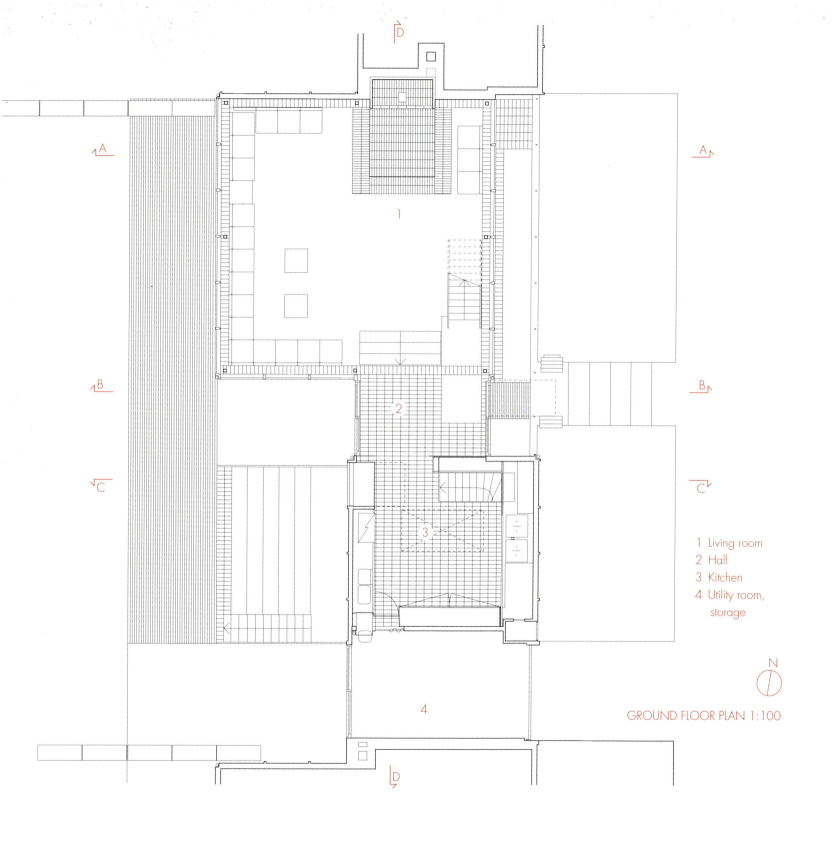

D

A

A

B

B

C

C

1

2

3

4

1 Living room
2 Hall
3 Kitchen
4 Utility room,
   storage

N

GROUND FLOOR PLAN 1:100

D

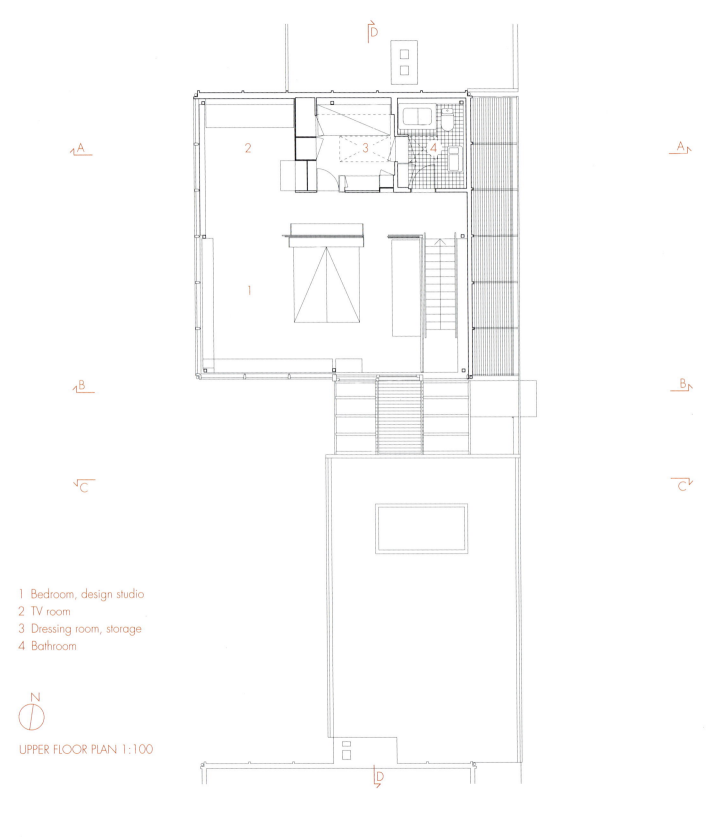

D

A   A

2

3

4

1

B   B

C   C

1 Bedroom, design studio
2 TV room
3 Dressing room, storage
4 Bathroom

N

UPPER FLOOR PLAN 1:100

D

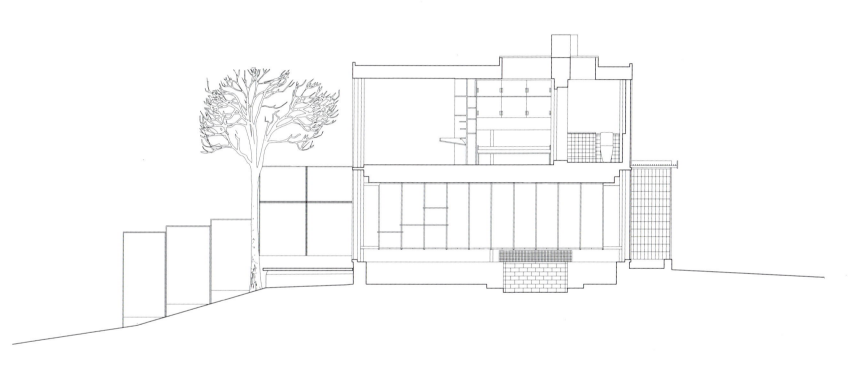

SECTION A–A 1:100

SECTION B–B 1:100

SECTION C-C 1:100

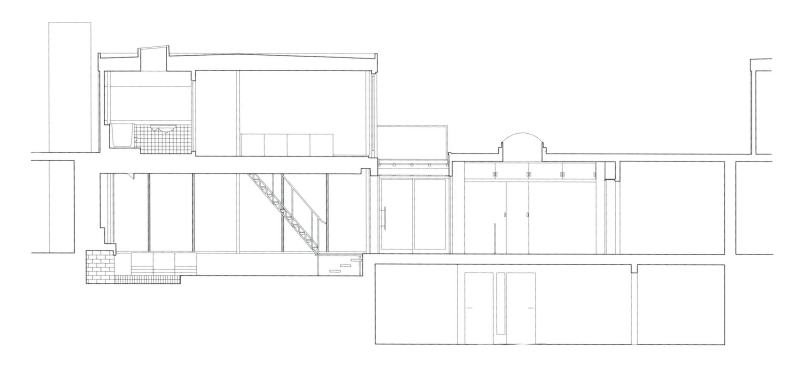

SECTION D–D 1:100

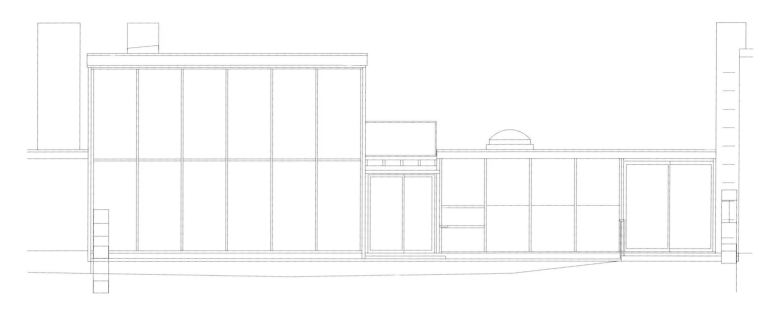

WEST ELEVATION

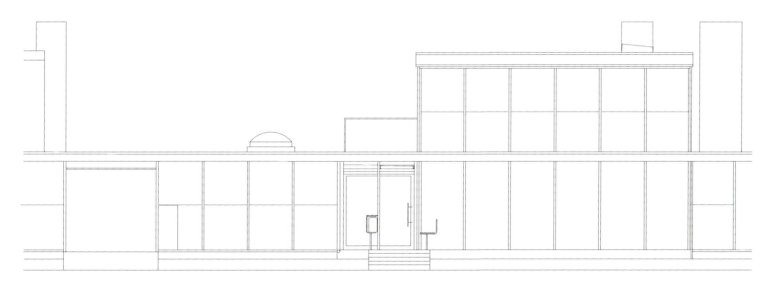

EAST ELEVATION

NOTES

ABBREVIATIONS
AHO Arkitektur- og designhøgskolen i Oslo
CIAM Congrès internationaux d'architecture moderne
CNS Christian Norberg-Schulz
FK Finn Fougner Kolstad
GPK Grete Prytz Kittelsen
HR Hanne Margrete Refsdal
NTH Norges Tekniske Høgskole
   (later incorporated in NTNU)
NTNU Norges teknisk-naturvinskapelige universitet
OAF Oslo Arkitektforening
PAGON Progressive arkitekters gruppe Oslo Norge
PBE Oslo kommune, Plan- og bygningsetaten
TM Terje Moe
SHKS Statens håndverks- og kunstindustriskole

1   Module from the Latin *modus*—unit of measurement: in architecture, a chosen unit of measurement that is repeated in the design of a building. For example, a module may be used to determine the intervals between load-bearing structural elements and/or the dimensions of windows and cladding materials. Some architectural styles emphasise the role of the module, while others may conceal it completely.

2   The architect Geir Grung, a former student and friend of Arne Korsmo, assisted Grete Prytz Kittelsen with the replacement of the entrance doors. He also planned the installation of a sliding door leading from the bedroom to the small balcony at upper-floor level. Subsequently he designed a carport on the other side of the road in 1972, after Prytz Kittelsen took over the garage for her design work.

3   Further examples of this trend in 1950s architecture are featured in Christoffer Harlang and Finn Monies, *Eget hus: om danske arkitekters egne huse I 1950'erne,* Copenhagen: Arkitektens Forlag, 2003.

4   10.4 x 21.4 cm with 0.5 cm grouting.

5   In Korsmo's presentation of the house, he stated that the veneer was mahogany, Arne Korsmo, "Hos arkitekt Arne Korsmo", *Byggekunst* 37, no. 7, 1955, p. 178, 181. Ulrich Hundhausen of the Norwegian Institute of Wood Technology has tested samples of the material. In his opinion, the veneer is not mahogany but is most probably teak. Written communication, 4 February 2011.

6   Norsk Flyindustri AS, Arne Korsmo and Christian Norberg-Schulz, "Tremannsbolig ved to av dem", *Byggekunst* 37, no. 7, 1955, p.173.

7   The teak shelves appear to be of the same thickness as the staircase treads, but are in fact thinner but edged with thick solid teak mouldings. The staircase treads however are solid teak, as is the low table in the seating area next to the fireplace.

8   "Hos arkitekt Arne Korsmo", pp.174–176.

9   Jacob Tostrup AS had a shop with several large display windows at street level next to the Parliament building on the main shopping street in Oslo, Karl Johans gate, as well as a workshop on the fifth floor. GPK remembered that two liveried men were employed to accompany visitors in the lift. The company also had a workshop with large metal presses at Alfheimgården, at Pilestredet 27 in Oslo.

10   The proofing press was later given to Gunnar S Gundersen.

11   Students who in the autumn of 2002 wrote essays about Planetveien 12 were interested in this topic and considered that "the architect tried to achieve too much". "Writing course" led by Elisabeth Tostrup, autumn 2002, Department of Architecture, Oslo School of Architecture and Design (AHO).

12   Korsmo, "Hos arkitekt Arne Korsmo", p.181. In his book about Korsmo, Norberg-Schulz also quotes Korsmo's rapturous description of the creamy grey shantung silk curtains at the Farnsworth House outside Chicago. Christian Norberg-Schulz, *Arne Korsmo,* Norske arkitekter 3, Oslo: Universitetsforl, 1986, pp. 67–69.

13   Korsmo, "Hos arkitekt Arne Korsmo", p.181. Also in conversation with GPK, 21 August 2006. Plan dated 7 February 1954, private collection.

14   The drawing for the wide teak steps shows the tread as being made of laminboard edged with only a thin layer of teak. The author's notes dating from 3 April 2008 describe the treads as made from 40 mm high x 70 mm wide pieces of solid teak glued together with 32 mm wide cross-tongue joints. The planks of solid teak in the low table in front of the fireplace are 38 mm high and glued together without cross tongues.

15   A photograph shows a similar wicker deckchair on the terrace of the 1958 home of Danish architect Halldor Gunløgsson, Harlang and Monies, *Eget hus: om danske arkitekters egne huse i 1950'erne,* p. 84.

16   Odd Kjeld Østbye in conversation, 27 January 2005.

17   Østbye was referring to the exhibition Grete Korsmo: works in silver and enamel works, and Arne Korsmo: architecture and furniture in Galerie Artek, Helsinki, autumn 1953. See also Thomas Flor et al., *Grete Prytz Kittelsen emalje—design,* Oslo: Gyldendal, 2008, p. 275. Hanne Refsdal until recently had photographs of this model with the various arrangements of furniture, HR, conversation, 25 January 2007.

18   City of Oslo, Agency for Planning and Building Services (PBE), Planetveien 10, 12, 14, row of three attached houses with garages, card 1, image 5, "Declaration", Oslo City Clerk's Office, 31 May 1954, point 3.

19   Presumably these outdoor partitions were erected with the neighbours' consent. Drawing "Dividing wall between attached houses B and C 1:50 and 1:1" dated 15 August 56, signed K.

20   Arne Korsmo, "Alfredheim pikehjem," *Byggekunst* 34, no.12, 1952.

21   Anna Maria Norberg-Schulz, conversation 18 January 2005.

22   See also Store Norske Leksikon www.snl.no/ nbl_biografi/Christian_Norberg-Schulz/utdypning Norberg-Schulz's publications included *Intentions in Architecture, Genius Loci. Towards a Phenomenology of Architecture, Mellom jord og himmel* and *Stedskunst. Et sted å være.* He was also the author of a book about Arne Korsmo, published in 1986.

23   See, for example, Johan Ellefsen, "Hvad er tidsmessig arkitektur?", *Byggekunst* 9, no. 11, 1927.

24   Johan Tømmervåg, "Hvem skapte byen?", in *Årbok for Nordmøre 2009,* ed. Nordmøre historielag, Kristiansund: Historielaget, 2009.

25   From September 1949 to May 1950. Arne Korsmo later held a second Fulbright scholarship for 1959–1960 to carry out research at the Massachusetts Institute of Technology (MIT). According to the Fulbright office in Norway, he was in the USA from February to July 1960. Cathrine Schrumpf, written communication, 25 July 2007.

26   Originally named Chicago School of Design, the institute was renamed in 1944.

27   Edgar Kaufmann Jr was invited to visit the four Nordic countries during the summer of 1948 in order to select examples of the applied arts for a joint Nordic exhibition at MoMA. For Nordic designers, Kaufmann's visit was a disappointment: "He found the Danes traditional, the Swedish stiff and the Norwegians immature. Only in Finland did he find some items of interest", according to Knut Greve, "Eksperiment eller tradisjon", *Bonytt* 10, 1950, p. 16, See also Håkon Stenstadvold, "Nederlag", *Bonytt,* 1949, p. 9. The exhibition never took place, but Kaufmann had

noticed work by both the Korsmos and invited GPK to participate in the "Good Design" exhibition in 1951. Flor et al., *Grete Prytz Kittelsen emalje—design*, 68.

28   Arne Korsmo, "Til unge arkitektsinn", *A5- Meningsblad for unge arkitekter* 9, nos. 1–2, 1956, p. 41.

29   "Det nasjonale og det Internasjonale I moderne arkitektur", *Arkkitehti* 64, nos. 7–8, 1967, p.13.

30   See also Alexandra Tyng, *Beginnings Louis I Kahn's Philosophy of Architecture*, New York: Wiley, 1984, p.185, Tyng's book about her father Louis Kahn. According to Refsdal, Suneko visited Norway, including Trondheim, in around 1965, conversation 25 April 2009.

31   GPK, conversation 1 February 2007.

32   GPK, in conversation, several times between 1994 and 2007. Korsmo and Farnsworth stayed up talking long into the night, with Prytz Kittelsen finally leaving them and going to bed. According to Flor et al., it was van der Rohe and Korsmo who stayed up late discussing architectural theory. However GPK told me more than once that it was Farnsworth and Korsmo, which seems to me to have been just as likely.

33   901, Washington Street, now Abbot Kinney Street, in Santa Monica, Los Angeles, not to be confused with the current Eames Office Gallery at 2665, Main Street.

34   Eames Demetrios, *An Eames Primer*, New York: Universe Publishing, 2001, p. 136.

35   *An Eames Primer*, p. 136. During the war, Eames had gained experience of mass production when using moulded plywood to manufacture splints to protect injured limbs.

36   Esther McCoy et al., *Blueprints for Modern Living History and Legacy of the Case Study Houses*, Los Angeles: Museum of Contemporary Art, 1989, p. 19.

37   Esther McCoy, *Case Study Houses 1945–1962*, Los Angeles, CA: Hennessey & Ingalls, 1977, p. 4.

38   McCoy et al., *Blueprints for Modern Living History and Legacy of the Case Study Houses*, pp. 18–19. Pre-war exponents of Modernism in Southern California included important architects such as Rudolph Schindler and Richard Neutra.

39   Cited in McCoy, *Case Study Houses 1945–1962*, p. 5. See also McCoy et al., *Blueprints for Modern Living History and Legacy of the Case Study Houses*, p. 51.

40   Jørn Utzon, "Platforms and Plateaus: Ideas of a Danish Architect/Source: *Zodiac*, 1962, vol. 10, pp. 112–140. Details: Ill, Plans, Port", *Zodiac*, 1962. The Utzons also greatly valued the time spent with the Korsmos

during this trip, see Norberg-Schulz, *Arne Korsmo.*, and Flor et al., *Grete Prytz Kittelsen emalje—Design*. GPK always maintained close contact with the Utzons, speaking regularly on the telephone until Jørn Utzon's death in November 2008.

41   Book 4 in Riksarkivet (National Archives), PA-0249 Prytz, Torolf (Gullsmedfirmaet Tostrup, J A/S), F-2. deposit, 1864–1956, 0020-04. These notes and draft letters to various contacts in the United States following the Korsmos' return to Norway provide insight into the professional relationships and friendships that were made. Correspondence between Korsmo and Mies is also archived in the Library of Congress, Washington DC under Mies van der Rohe.

42   Arne Korsmo and Christian Norberg-Schulz, "Charles Eames som arkitekt", *Bonytt* 11, 1951; Arne Korsmo and Christian Norberg-Schulz, "Mies van der Rohe", *Byggekunst* 34, no. 5, 1952, pp. 85–91.

43   GPK was one of the founders of the World Craft Council in New York in 1964 and in 1986 was appointed an honorary member.

44   Later the cane sofa was replaced by two plain sofas with mattress-style seat cushions and backs covered with a grey fabric, "A Bygdöy, presso Oslo", *Domus*, no. 302, 1955, p. 35.

45   Arne Korsmo, "Romeksperimenter: Innredning av egen leilighet på Bygdøy", *Byggekunst* 34, no. 3, 1952, p. 42. "Home and Dwelling" was not an actual department at the college, but was rather an umbrella term covering two departments: i) the department officially known as Timber-based Design (which included the furniture workshop), which was headed by Korsmo; and Building Design, headed by the architect Arne Vesterlid. The Department of Building Design focused on house-building and provided the foundation training necessary for enrolment on the course leading to the nationally-recognised qualification in architecture. This latter course (SAK) was established in autumn 1945.

46   The Dutch painter Pieter Cornelis (Piet) Mondrian (1872–1944) was a key figure in the artistic movement De Stijl, founded by Theo van Doesburg in 1917. Mondrian's paintings and principles were an important point of reference for Bauhaus-inspired teaching in architecture.

47   Korsmo, "Til unge arkitektsinn", p. 49.

48   The lecture "The connection between contemporary art and architecture" has been translated into Norwegian and extracts reproduced with commentary in Harald Klem, "Arkitekturdebatten", *Byggekunst* 29, no.10,

1948. The commentary links Giedion's lecture with that of Richard J Neutra, which was delivered at the following meeting of the Oslo Association of Architects (OAF).

49   Odd Kjeld Østbye, in conversation, 27 January 2005. See also Espen Johnsen, "Giedion, Ciam og etableringen av Pagon (1945–50)", in *Brytninger. Norsk arkitektur 1945–65*, ed. Espen Johnsen, Oslo: Nasjonalmuseet for kunst, arkitektur og design, 2010.

50   Østbye in conversation, 27 January 2005. According to Østbye, Fehn and Grung were unable to attend because they were too busy working on the museum project at Maihaugen.

51   Østbye in conversation, 27 January 2005.

52   Rameses II, also known as Rameses the Great, the pharaoh who ruled Egypt from 1279–1213 BC In 2009, one of the books still left after Korsmo was an original copy of Howard Carter and AC Mace, *The Tomb of Tut-Ankh-Amen: Discovered by the Late Earl of Carnarvon and Howard Carter*, London: Cassel, 1923.

53   Østbye in conversation, 27 January 2005.

54   Pagon, "Om rommet i arkitekturen", *Byggekunst* 34, nos. 6–7, 1952. "Bolig?", *Byggekunst* 34, nos. 6–7, 1952. "Hjemmets mekano", *Byggekunst* 34, nos. 6–7 1952.

55   Nina Berre and Elisabeth Tostrup, "Pagon og modernismens reformulering", *Byggekunst* 88, no. 5, 2006.

56   Pagon, "Om rommet i arkitekturen", *Byggekunst* 34, nos. 6–7, 1952, p. 101.

57   Sverre Fehn, Geir Grung, Håkon Mjelva, Chr Norberg-Schulz, Odd Østbye, "Gruppe 5", *A5-meningsblad for unge arkitekter* 9, nos. 1–2, 1956; Korsmo, "Til unge arkitektsinn".

58   Gunnar S Gundersen, "En oppgave i samarbeidets tegn", *A5-meningsblad for unge arkitekter* 9, nos. 1–2, 1956.

59   Statens håndverks- og kunstindustriskole, *årsmelding 1952–1953, 1953–1954*, Oslo: SHKS, 1955, p. 11.

60   Arne Korsmo, "Grunnlaget og prinsipper for opplæringen ved fagavdeling tre", in *Statens håndverks-og kunstindustriskole, årsmelding 1952–1953, 1953–1954*, SHKS, 1955, p. 31.

61   "Til unge arkitektsinn", pp. 44–45.

62   Jacob Tostrup Prytz, "Bolig- og hjeminnredning", in *Statens håndverks- og kunstindustriskole årsmelding 1952–1953, 1953–1954*, ed. SHKS, Oslo: SHKS, 1955, (various pagings) p. 6.

63   SHKS, ed. *Statens håndverks-og kunstindustriskole, årsmelding 1952–1953, 1953–1954*, Oslo: SHKS, 1955, in the paragraph "Nye opplæringsmetoder".

Precise references are difficult to provide, since the booklet is only partially paginated and lacks a table of contents. In addition, passages are not attributed to specific authors and there are no clear divisions between the various articles.

64 Norberg-Schulz, *Arne Korsmo*, p. 79.

65 GPK, in conversation, 11 February 2008.

66 "Praktiske romstudier" in SHKS, *Statens håndsverks-og kunstindustriskole, årsmelding 1952–1953, 1953–1954*, (various pagings) p. 64.

67 This was also not dissimilar to Kaare Klint's teaching methods at the furniture department of Kunstakademiets Arkitektskole in Copenhagen during the 1920s, Nils-Ole Lund, *Nordisk arkitektur*, 2nd ed., Copenhagen: Arkitektens Forlag, 1993, pp. 59–61.

68 "Praktisk eksperimentoppgave 1953, 48 m² leiligheten" in SHKS, *Statens håndsverks-og kunstindustriskole, årsmelding 1952–1953, 1953–1954*, unpaginated.

69 Norberg-Schulz, *Arne Korsmo*, p. 73.

70 Jon Bræenne, Eirik T Bøe, and Astrid Skjerven, *Arne Korsmo: Arkitektur og design*, Oslo: Universitetsforlaget, 2004, p. 169.

71 TM, in conversation, 16 October 2005. Terje Moe was a student of Korsmo and also worked with Korsmo in Trondheim from 1958 to 1966. He became a professor at the Norwegian University of Science and Technology (NTNU—formerly the Norwegian Institute of Technology or NTH) in Trondheim in 1987, working in the same department as where Korsmo had been a professor. See also Gaute Baalsrud, "Terje Moe: Huset og mannen", *Arkitektur i Norge - årbok*, 2006. Hanne Refsdal owned this model for many years until she moved house in 1991. The model is now in the collections of the National Museum of Art, Architecture and Design.

72 Arne Korsmo, "Treavdelingen ved Statens håndverks- og industriskole", *Byggekunst* 34, no.12, 1952, p. 274.

73 TM, in conversation, 16 October 2005.

74 HR, in conversation, 25 February 2007.

75 Gundersen, "En oppgave i samarbeidets tegn", pp. 56–57.

76 FK, In conversation 14 May 2011.

77 Cited in Norberg-Schulz, *Arne Korsmo*, p. 81.

78 Cited in *Arne Korsmo*, p. 81.

79 In *Arne Korsmo*, p. 65.

80 HR, in conversation, 25 January 2007.

81 Richard Weston, *Utzon: Inspiration, Vision, Architecture*, Hellerup: Edition Bløndal, 2002, p. 28.

82 Letter from Utzon thanking Moe for some photographs Moe had sent him, which were taken by Alexey Zaitzow while the Korsmos were living in Løchenveien. The author saw the letter in Terje Moe's possession on 7 February 2007, but unfortunately it has now been lost.

83 GPK, conversation, 4 November 2007.

84 Kaare Stang, "Z for Zaitzow", A bit of magic, Norge: Norsk Filminstitutt, 2007; "Z for Zaitzow", DVD.

85 HR, in conversation, 25 January 2007.

86 TZ, conversations during summer 2007. Tatjana Zaitzow also studied architecture during Korsmo's time at NTH and was employed for some time as a tutor in his Department of Architectural Design II. From 1978, she devoted her energy to puppet theatre, becoming artistic director of the Petrusjka Theatre in Trondheim. In an email dated 27 May 2011, she wrote: "what lit a little architectural spark in me, was when Korsmo, on one of his many visits to our house when I was growing up, showed us photographs of student work at the National College of Applied Arts. There were figures that were folded, twisted and shaped out of paper. That was something that inspired me very much in some of my own student projects some years later at NTH. Korsmo and Papa were also very interested in the Bauhaus, and I remember seeing several photographs from it."

87 See also Flor et al., *Grete Prytz Kittelsen emalje-design*; Karianne Bjellås Gilje, ed. *Grete Prytz Kittelsen: The Art of Enamel Design*, New York, NY: WW Norton & Company, 2012.

88 Sissel Aabel Aaby, in conversation, 12 May 2011. The company J Tostrup ceased operations in 1991.

89 Norberg-Schulz, *Arne Korsmo*, pp. 41, 45. The couple divorced in 1944.

90 Coincidentally, Arne Korsmo made a proposal (dated 4 December 1935) to develop the Juel's family property, "Lønnhaugen". Book 1 in the Norwegian National Archives, PA-0249 Prytz, Torolf (Gullsmedfirmaet Tostrup, J A/S), F-2. deposit 1864–1956, 0020-04.

91 Korsmo quoted in Norberg-Schulz, *Arne Korsmo*, p. 31.

92 The silver-plating was applied to a nickel silver base, Sissel Aabel Aaby in conversation, 17 April 2009. At that time, the cost of the metal was significant in comparison with that of labour, while the opposite is the case today. This is a major reason why the cutlery set has not re-entered production. After the war, anyone wanting to purchase new silverware was required to provide 50 per cent of the silver used for its production

(frequently this requirement was met by handing in older items that could be melted down). See also Astrid Skjerven, "'Material, Technique, and Requirements': Arne Korsmo's Flatware", *Scandinavian Journal of design history* 6, 1996.

93 Korsmo in Karl Teigen, "Nye sølvarbeider", *Bonytt* 9, nos. 5–6, 1949, p. 85. Korsmo's name appears under a kind of appendix to Teigen's article.

94 GPK, in conversation, 24 March 2006.

95 GPK, in conversation, 24 March 2006.

96 GPK, in conversation, 28 February 2007. Also "C.I.A.M. 9 Aix-en-Provence, La Charte de l'habitat", *L'Architecture d'Aujourd'hui* 24, no. 49, 1953, and Flor et al., *Grete Prytz Kittelsen emalje—design*, p. 60.

97 *Grete Prytz Kittelsen emalje—design*, p. 89.

98 Maire Gullichsen was heiress to the Ahlstrom fortune, which had its roots in a highly successful pulp, paper and timber business. By the 1950s, Ahlstrom was the leading industrial conglomerate in Finland and was expanding rapidly.

99 The final drawings submitted for building consent were approved on 24 May 1954, PBE card 1, p. 6.

100 Since 1950, GPK had been working with the Norwegian Institute for Industrial Research (SI). Her sister's husband, Bjarne Andvord Tønnesen, was employed as a civil engineer at the Institute, where he worked with the chemical engineer Johannes O Müller on the production of high-quality enamels in different colours that could be used on different types of metal. One result of this collaboration was that it became possible to enamel larger objects, cf. Flor et al..

101 Korsmo was architect for the refurbishment of the public areas at the Britannia Hotel, a project he completed in collaboration with Terje Moe between 1961 and 1963. It was an exquisite piece of work that included, on the ground floor, the entrance, reception area and the restaurant "Hjørnet" and, in the basement, the bar, cloakrooms and toilets. The materials used included Carrara marble, various types of glass, Cuban mahogany, copper and brass. As usual with Korsmo, he involved a team with many different skills. Apart from himself and Moe as architects, there were the interior designers Bernard Witte and Liv Arvesen, as well as Gunnar S Gundersen and Grete Prytz, who both contributed within their respective areas of expertise. See also Arne Korsmo and Terje Moe, "Ombygging av Britannia Hotel i Trondheim", *Byggekunst* 45, no. 5, 1963.

102 HR, in conversation 25 February 2007.

103 Sverre Kittelsen (1915–2002) was a senior executive and legal adviser at Norsk Hydro, a major Norwegian industrial concern.

104 Such relationships are considered in Whitney Chadwick and Isabelle De Courtivron, *Significant others: creativity and intimate partnership*, London: Thames and Hudson, 1993, and were the topic of the Nordic symposium "Pardesign" [lit. "Couples Design"], at the National Museum of Art, Architecture and Design, Oslo, 4–5 June 2009.

105 HR, conversation 25 January 2007.

106 GPK, in conversation 15 June 2003.

107 PBE, card 1, b3 dated 14 May 1952 and 1, b5, dated 16 June 1952.

108 Meeting of Oslo City Council on 7 November 1952, letter from Oslo Planning Department, 21 November 1952.

109 PBE Sheet 1/4, signed Christian Norberg-Schulz 5 May 1952.

110 PBE Sheet 1/10 signed Harald Wildhagen. The approval is dated 11 August 1953. The three sets of plans for the planning application were dated, respectively, 13 March 1952, 13 March 1953 and 13 April1954. The documents relating to the neighbours' objections, as well as to the hearings before the building authority, confirm that the application was submitted in 1952.

111 29 June 1953. Otherwise recommended for approval, J Nissen.

112 The time spent by CNS in the United States had furnished him with an additional incentive to see the project realised. At Harvard he had met an Italian woman, Anna Maria De Dominicis, with whom he formed a serious relationship. After she had returned to Rome and he had returned to Oslo, CNS wrote to her describing the project and its progress. GPK told me in conversation on 15 June 2003 that CNS wanted to have a modern home ready for De Domenicis on their marriage. The couple married in Rome on 19 February 1955. Immediately afterwards they travelled by train to Germany, where they took delivery of a new Volkswagen Beetle (Norway having recently lifted its ban on car imports). They then drove north to Oslo and moved into Planetveien 14, which was just about habitable.

113 Is the date on the proposal erroneous, perhaps because someone wrote 1953 out of habit, instead of 1954? It is remarkable that it appears to have taken over a year for receipt of the drawing to have been officially recorded by the municipal authorities. An alternative explanation may be that the steel structure itself had not been changed, merely the floor plan for the upper floor?

114 "Arkitekturens kanon: de tolv viktigste byggene i norsk etterkrigstid", *Morgenbladet*, 30 November 2007.

115 JA Bonnevie, "Hvordan kan vi bygge i dag?", *Bonytt* 12, 1952, p. 4. See also "Nytt om småhusbygging", *Bonytt* 16, 1956.

116 The gross ground floor area of the two-storey volume is 57 m², while that of the single-storey wing is approximately 50 m².

117 Bonnevie, "Hvordan kan vi bygge i dag?", p. 6.

118 "Hvordan kan vi bygge i dag?", p. 11.

119 PBE, card 1, b15.

120 PA M Mellbye, "Kan vi bo og trives på 80-90 m²?", *Bonytt* 12, 1952, p. 20.

121 Helge Abrahamsen, *Nordiske småhus*, Oslo: Nordisk byggedag, 1958.

122 Kjell Lund, "Norge", in *Nordiske småhus*, ed. Helge Abrahamsen, Oslo: Nordisk byggedag, 1958, pp. 140–141.

123 "Norge", p. 141.

124 "Norge", p. 141.

125 "Hus og glass," *Byggekunst* 40, no. 1, 1958, p. 17.

126 In the history of twentieth century architecture in Norway, Knut Knutsen was the polar opposite of Kormso. While Knutsen promoted an architecture that was based on and renewed traditional Norwegian architecture, Korsmo was known as the champion of a more international orientation. Kjell Lund was not known as a typical Knutsen disciple, however. He studied in Trondheim, not under Knutsen in Oslo, and represents an intermediate position—Norwegian Brutalism and Structuralism—which combined Le Corbusier-inspired architecture in concrete and masonry with traditional Norwegian wooden architecture. The English architects Alison and Peter Smithson coined the term Brutalism in 1954. The word derives from the French *béton brut* (raw concrete), which was how Le Corbusier described concrete surfaces bearing the imprint of the wood or plywood formwork into which the concrete had been poured. Many of Le Corbusier's post-war buildings were constructed using this technique.

127 Written communication from the architect Gaute Baalsrud, 14 August 2009. Baalsud had been present in Rinnan's office in 1956 when this telephone conversation took place.

128 James A Lees and Walter J Clutterbuck, *Tre i Norge: ved to av dem*, Oslo: Johan Grundt Tanum, 1949. The book was published in English in 1882, *Three in Norway*, London: Longmans, Green & Co., 1882, and in Norwegian in 1884. Since then it has been republished more than 15 times in Norwegian and more than ten times in English. The title of the *Byggekunst* article is also appropriate because the article features two of the three row houses.

129 *Tre i Norge: ved to av dem*, p. 8.

130 Korsmo and Norberg-Schulz, "Tremannsbolig ved to av dem".

131 GPK, in conversation, 15 February 2005.

132 GPK, in conversation, 15 June 2003. The author accompanied Grete Prytz Kittelsen on a visit to "Solhaugen", Ivar Aasens Road 14, on 13 April 2004. The living room at "Solhaugen" measures 690 x 720 cm. Hilda Prytz, née Tostrup, was the granddaughter of the founder of the goldsmithing firm, Jacob H Tostrup.

133 GPK, in conversation 5 September 2002.

134 GPK interviewd by Maria Landrø Evensen for "Grete Prutz Kittelsen—inspirert og inspirerende", published in the Ullern newspaper *Akersposten*, Friday 21 September 2001, pp. 8–9, in connection with GPK's contribution to the exhibition "Inspirert design", Kunstindustrimuseet, Oslo, autumn 2001.

135 P Chr Asbjørnsen and Jørgen Moe, "Småguttene som traff trollene på Hedalsskogen", in *Samlede eventyr* Oslo: Gyldendal, 1936.

136 Arne Korsmo, "Japan og Vestens arkitektur", *Byggekunst* 38, no. 3, 1956, p. 74. Korsmo referred to the books Werner Blaser, *Tempel und Teehaus in Japan*, Olten: Urs-Graf-Verlag, 1955, and Kakuzô Okakura and Elise Grilli, *The Book of Tea*, Rutland, VT: Tuttle, 1956. The latter, which was written in English, was first published in 1906 and was subsequently published in countless editions in many languages.

137 Korsmo, "Japan og Vestens arkitektur", p. 74.

138 "Japan og Vestens arkitektur", p. 71.

139 "Japan og Vestens arkitektur", p. 71. To accompany his article, Korsmo shows photographs of wood constructions by the architects Greene & Greene in California and of Aalto's sauna for Villa Mairea in Finland as examples of interpretations of Japanese architecture.

140 "Japan og Vestens arkitektur", p. 74.

141 "Japan og Vestens arkitektur", p. 74.

142 Nils-Ole Lund, "Japanske bondehuse," *Byggekunst* 45, no. 2, 1963. As a Dane, he must also have seen a strong parallel with the large thatched roofs that are typical of traditional Danish farmhouses.

143 Gullik Kollandsrud, "Modulens hjemland," *Byggekunst* 41, no. 2, 1959. The plan is reproduced from Werner Blaser's book *Tempel und Teehaus in Japan*, 1955. A first edition of this book was found among Korsmo's effects after his death, along with a copy of an exceptionally fine book about the Katsura Imperial Villa in Kyoto. Written by Kenzo Tange in collaboration with Walter Gropius, this book was inscribed: "To Mr. Arne Korsmo—with respect and friendship, Kenzo Tange, 1 September 1960." Tange and Korsmo knew each other through CIAM.

144 Emil Korsmo, *Anatomy of Weeds: Anatomical Description of 95 Weed Species with 2050 Original Drawings*, Oslo: Grøndahl, 1954.

145 Norberg-Schulz, *Arne Korsmo*, pp. 28–29.

146 TM, in conversation, 16 October 2005.

147 The original exists typed in black on unbleached white paper.

148 Korsmo in PAGON, "Hjemmets mekano", p. 110.

149 Korsmo in "Hjemmets mekano", p. 110.

150 "Hjemmets mekano", p. 110.

151 "Hjemmets mekano", p. 111.

152 "Hjemmets mekano", p. 112.

153 "Hjemmets mekano", p. 112.

154 "Hjemmets mekano", p. 112.

155 Gennaro Postiglione, "Arne Korsmo eget hjem. A traditional house", in *Arne Korsmo—Knut Knutsen. Due Maestri del Nord*, Nicola Flora, Paolo Giardiello, and Gennaro Postiglione, Rome: Officina edizioni, 1999, p. 65.

156 "Praktiske romstudier" in SHKS, *Statens håndsverks- og kunstindustriskole, årsmelding 1952–1953, 1953–1954*, (several pagings, p. 64). In the 80 m² apartment it is difficult to detect the presence of a 60 cm module, even though this forms the basis of the apartment's design. For example, the length of a standard bed is not compatible with a 60 cm module.

157 Arne Remlov, "48 m² leilighet", *Bonytt*, 1954, p. 38. Several elements in the interior of Planetveien came from the experimental apartments constructed at SHKS: parts of the kitchen interior and the wall of cupboards containing the fold-out beds in the dressing room on the upper floor.

158 This was a problem when Jacob T Prytz wanted to donate a grand piano to the Korsmos. Since the couple did not want to have it in their living room, Prytz donated it instead to SHKS. GPK, in conversation, 1 February 2007.

159 "Schindler-Shelters", *American Architect* 146, May 1935 "Schindler-Shelters", RM Schindler, "Reference Frames in Space", *Architect and Engineer* 165, no. 1, 1946, and Jin-Ho Park, "An Integral Approach to Design Strategies and Construction Systems—RM Schindler's "Schindler Shelters"," *Journal of Architectural Education* 58, November, 2004.

160 Conversation, 15 February 2005.

161 Such a drawing at a scale of 1:200, dated 1 March 1955, is signed AK and BW (Bernard Witte).

162 Bjørn Wærenskjold, in conversation, June 2008. Grete Prytz Kittelsen stated that she had never understood what "the Home Meccano method" really involved.

163 Norberg-Schulz, *Arne Korsmo*, p. 73.

164 Park, "An Integral Approach to Design Strategies and Construction Systems—RM Schindler's "Schindler Shelters", *Journal of Architectural Education* 58, pp. 30–31.

165 Jorge Otero-Pailos, "Norberg-Schulz' hus: en moderne søken etter hjemmets visuelle mønster", *Byggekunst* 88, no. 7, 2006. Originally presented as a lecture at the Fehn Symposium at Domkirkeodden, Hamar, Norway, 11–13 May 2006

166 Schindler had also worked for Wright throughout the 1920s from the time when Wright became involved in designing the new Imperial Hotel in Tokyo.

167 Korsmo and Norberg-Schulz, "Tremannsbolig ved to av dem", p. 172. According to Professor Per Kristian Larsen at the Norwegian University of Science and Technology (NTNU), hollow structural sections were not generally available in Norway at the time the houses in Planetveien were built (except for circular hollow sections), 18 January 2011. Several undated detailed drawings in the Planetveien archive show cross-sections of rolled steel sections welded together: alternatively a pair of angle sections welded together at the corners, or two channel sections welded facing each other to form an 8 x 8 cm four-sided section. It should be possible to see the welding joints, but no doubt care was taken to grind down, fill, and polish them. This means that it is impossible to see the joints without removing the paint, and the columns have the appearance of rectangular hollow sections with slightly rounded corners. Closer inspection suggests that they are indeed formed of two angle sections welded together.

168 Jorge Otero-Pailos, "Norberg-Schulz' hus: en moderne søken etter hjemmets visuelle mønster", *Byggekunst* 88, no. 7, 2006.

169 GPK, in conversation, 15 February 2005.

170 TM, in conversation, 15 February 2005.

171 A thermal bridge (or cold bridge) is an area of the building fabric that has poorer thermal insulation than the surrounding parts of the fabric, resulting in a local loss of heat. Or to put it another way, the cold penetrates the internal space, whether through the roof, walls or floor, with consequences such as condensation and structural damage. In Norway, where there are significant differences between internal and external temperatures during the course of a year, "thermal bridges" are an important issue when designing a building.

172 The drawing for the studwork in the kitchen wing specifies two sizes of stud (2 1/2" x 6" and 2" x 3") to be installed alternately, with 2" x 3" diagonal bracings in the corners and 1 1/2" x 3" noggins running at half height. This created a base to which the fibre cement panels used for the facade could be fastened, without unnecessarily degrading the insulation (drawing dated 12.8.54, RM + section 1:50). Lightweight framing or studwork according to the "balloon-frame" method became common in Norway after the First World War. It replaced the far stronger, heavier framework that had been developed during the seventeenth century and that was used until around 1950. As mentioned previously, 2" x 4" lumber was recommended for small house construction.

173 I was happy to find confirmation from the Dutch architecture critic and author Hans Ibelings of the existence of this phenomenon that similar ideas and solutions can arise at the same time even though the creators have no direct contact. Lecture at the Oslo School of Architecture and Design on 19 January 2011 in connection with Ibelings' forthcoming book about the history of modern architecture. He cites in support of this view, among others, H G Barnett, *Innovation. The Basis of Cultural Change*, 1st ed., New York, Toronto, London: McGraw-Hill Book Company, 1953, in the chapter "The Cultural Background", p. 44.

174 Hanne Refsdal describes Arne Korsmo's ability to reorient his thinking as almost extreme and his sensory perception as extremely acute. One time they were out shooting with Utzon but did not have a dog with them. Korsmo however could sense the grouse almost like a hunting dog—and they succeeded in bagging a

grouse. Another time Korsmo got out of the car in the middle of the mountains and sniffed in all directions to find out whether there were foxes or other animals nearby. After ascertaining that no other animals were in evidence, he allowed his huskies, Atki and Sappok, who were completely uncontrollable in the presence of other animals, out of the car. In more cultural or spiritual contexts, Korsmo had a formidable ability to absorb new ideas and new associations, whether in music, mathematics or other fields. Korsmo was a voracious reader, but never actually finished a book. After he had read the foreword and a few pages, he would become lost in ideas inspired by what he had read. HR, in conversation, 28 April 2008 and 31 May 2011.

175 Gennaro Postiglione, "Arne Korsmos eget hjem. A traditional house" in eds. Nicola Flora, Paolo Giardello, and Gennaro Postiglione, *Arne Korsmo— Knut Knutsen. Due maestri del Nord*, Architettura Progetto 20, Roma: Officina Edizioni, 1999, pp. 46–71.

176 Astrid Skjerven, "Ny helhet", in *Arne Korsmo. Arkitektur og design*, eds. Jon Brænne, Eirik T Bøe and Astrid Skjerven, Oslo Universitetsforlaget, 2004, pp.171–174.

177 Pierre Chareau et al., *La maison de verre Pierre Chareau*, Tokyo: ADA Edita, 1988, p. 6.

178 Lund, *Nordisk arkitektur*, p. 63.

179 *Nordisk arkitektur*, pp. 26, 27, 103.

180 *Gesamtkunstwerk* (or "allkunstverk" in Norwegian) is a term used to describe a work of art that makes use of all or many forms of art. The term was used by the composer Richard Wagner in his 1849 essay "Art and Revolution", in which he describes in detail the unification of opera and drama, whereby individual artistic disciplines would be subordinated to, or integrated in, the pursuit of a greater common purpose. During the 1890s, the concept enjoyed a revival when painters and architects began to integrate different art forms to design exterior and interior architecture. Henry van de Velde played a significant role in this trend. He was a key figure in the Art Nouveau movement, and would later found the Grand-Ducal School of Arts and Crafts in Weimar. This was the predecessor of the Bauhaus, which was to be further developed by Walter Gropius.

181 GB, "Ukens portrett", *Dagbladet*, no. 163, 17 July 1937. "Romkunst" refers to the German *Raumkunst*.

182 GPK, in conversation, 2005, and many times thereafter.

BIBLIOGRAPHY

Abrahamsen, Helge, *Nordiske småhus*, Oslo: Nordisk byggedag,1958.

"Arkitekturens kanon: De tolv viktigste byggene i norsk etterkrigstid", *Morgenbladet*, 30 November 2007, appendix.

Asbjørnsen, P Chr and Jørgen Moe, "Småguttene som traff trollene på Hedalsskogen", *Samlede eventyr*. Oslo: Gyldendal, 1936.

Baalsrud, Gaute, "Terje Moe: Huset og mannen", *Arkitektur i Norge—årbok*, 2006, pp. 56–65.

Barnett, HG, *Innovation. The Basis of Cultural Change*, 1st ed., New York, Toronto, London: McGraw-Hill Book Company, 1953.

Berre, Nina and Elisabeth Tostrup, "Pagon og modernismens reformulering", *Byggekunst* 88, no. 5, 2006, pp. 24–26.

Blaser, Werner, *Tempel und Teehaus in Japan*, Olten: Urs-Graf-Verlag, 1955.

Bonnevie, JA, "Hvordan kan vi bygge i dag?", *Bonytt* 12, 1952, pp. 2–15.

"Nytt om småhusbygging", *Bonytt* 16, 1956, pp. 23–24.

Brænne, Jon, Eirik T Bøe, Astrid Skjerven, *Arne Korsmo: Arkitektur og design*. Oslo: Universitetsforlaget, 2004.

"A Bygdöy, presso Oslo", *Domus*, no. 302, January 1955, pp. 34–35.

"C.I.A.M. 9 Aix-en-Provence, La Charte de L'habitat", *L'Architecture d'Aujourd'hui* 24, no. 49, 1953, pp. IX–XI.

Carter, Howard, AC Mace, *The Tomb of Tut-Ankh-Amen: Discovered by the Late Earl of Carnarvon and Howard Carter*, London: Cassel, 1923.

Chareau, Pierre, Marc Vellay, Yukio Futagawa, Bernard Bauchet, *La maison de verre Pierre Chareau*, Tokyo: ADA Edita, 1988.

Demetrios, Eames, *An Eames Primer*, New York: Universe Publishing, 2001.

Ellefsen, Johan, "Hvad er tidsmessig arkitektur?" [in Norwegian], *Byggekunst* 9, November 1927, pp. 161–70.

Fehn, Sverre, Geir Grung, Håkon Mjelva, Chr. Norberg-Schulz, Odd Østbye, "Gruppe 5", *A5—meningsblad for unge arkitekter* 9, no. 1–2, 1956, pp. 67–80.

Flor, Thomas, Widar Halén, Astrid Skjerven, Jan-Lauritz Opstad, Karianne Bjellås Gilje, *Grete Prytz Kittelsen emalje—design*, Oslo: Gyldendal, 2008.

Flora, Nicola, Paolo Giardiello, Gennaro Postiglione, *Arne Korsmo—Knut Knutsen. Due maestri del Nord*, Architettura Progetto 20, Rome: Officina Edizioni, 1999.

GB, "Ukens portrett", *Dagbladet*, no. 163, 17 July 1937.

Gilje, Karianne Bjellås, ed., *Grete Prytz Kittelsen: The Art of Enamel Design*, New York, NY: WW Norton & Company, 2012.

Greve, Knut, "Eksperiment eller tradisjon", *Bonytt* 10, 1950, pp. 16–17.

Gundersen, Gunnar S, "En oppgave i samarbeidets tegn", *A5—meningsblad for unge arkitekter* 9, no. 1-2, 1956, pp. 56–59.

Harlang, Christoffer, Finn Monies, *Eget hus: Om danske*

arkitekters egne huse i 1950'erne, Copenhagen: Arkitektens Forlag, 2003.

Johnsen, Espen, "Giedion, Ciam og etableringen av Pagon (1945–50)", Brytninger. Norsk arkitektur 1945-65, ed. Espen Johnsen, Oslo: The National Museum for Art, Architecture and Design, 2010, pp. 66–81.

Klem, Harald, "Arkitekturdebatten", Byggekunst 29, no. 10, 1948, pp. 135–38.

Kollandsrud, Gullik, "Modulens hjemland", Byggekunst 41, no. 2, 1959, pp. 40–49.

Korsmo, Arne, "Alfredheim pikehjem", Byggekunst 34, no. 12, 1952, pp. 256–59.

"Det nasjonale og det Internasjonale i moderne arkitektur", Arkkitehti 64, no. 7–8, 1967, pp. 9–14.

"Grunnlaget og prinsipper for opplæringen ved fagavdeling tre", Statens Håndverks—Og Kunstindustriskole, årsmelding 1952–1953, 1953–1954, SHKS, 1955, (various pages) pp. 31–35.

"Hos arkitekt Arne Korsmo" [in Norwegian], Byggekunst 37, no. 7, 1955, pp. 174–83.

"Japan og Vestens arkitektur", Byggekunst 38, no. 3, 1956, pp. 70–75.

"Romeksperimenter: Innredning av egen leilighet på Bygdøy", Byggekunst 34, no. 3, 1952, pp. 40-42.

"Til unge arkitektsinn", A5—Meningsblad for unge arkitekter 9, no. 1–2, 1956, pp. 40–55.

"Treavdelingen ved Statens håndverks—og Industriskole", Byggekunst 34, no. 12, 1952, pp. 273–76.

Korsmo, Arne, Christian Norberg-Schulz, "Mies van der Rohe" [in Norwegian], Byggekunst 34, no. 5, 1952, pp. 85–91.

"Charles Eames som arkitekt", Bonytt 11, 1951, pp. 169–73.

"Tremannsbolig ved to av dem", Byggekunst 37, no. 7, 1955, pp. 169–73, 89.

Korsmo, Emil, Anatomy of Weeds: Anatomical Description of 95 Weed Species with 2050 Original Drawings, Oslo: Grøndahl, 1954.

Lees, James A, Walter J Clutterbuck, Three in Norway, London: Longmans, Green & Co., 1882.

Tre i Norge: ved to av dem, Oslo: Johan Grundt Tanum, 1949.

Lund, Kjell, "Hus og glass", Byggekunst 40, no. 1, 1958, pp. 14–18.

"Norge", Nordiske småhus, ed. Helge Abrahamsen, Oslo: Nordisk byggedag, 1958, pp. 140–42.

Lund, Nils-Ole, "Japanske bondehuse", Byggekunst 45, no. 2, 1963, pp. 50–55.

Nordisk arkitektur, 2nd ed., Copenhagen: Arkitektens Forlag, 1993.

McCoy, Esther, Case Study Houses 1945–1962, Los Angeles, California: Hennessey & Ingalls, 1977.

McCoy, Esther, Howard Singerman, Elizabeth AT Smith, Museum of Contemporary Art, Blueprints for Modern Living History and Legacy of the Case Study Houses, Los Angeles: Museum of Contemporary Art, 1989.

Mellbye, PAM, "Kan vi bo og trives på 80–90 m²?", Bonytt 12, 1952, pp. 16–20.

Korsmo, Arne and Terje Moe, "Ombygging av Britannia Hotel i Trondheim", Byggekunst 45, no. 5, 1963, pp. 130–33.

Norberg-Schulz, Christian, Arne Korsmo, Norske arkitekter 3, 1st ed., Oslo: Universitetsforlaget, 1986.

Okakura, Kakuzô, Elise Grilli, The Book of Tea, Rutland, Vermont: Tuttle, 1956.

Otero-Pailos, Jorge, "Norberg-Schulz' hus: En moderne søken etter hjemmets visuelle mønstre", [in Norwegian], Byggekunst 88, no. 7, 2006, pp. 10–17.

PAGON, "Bolig?", Byggekunst 34, no. 6–7, 1952, pp. 108–09.

"Hjemmets mekano", Byggekunst 34, no. 6–7, 1952, pp. 110–13.

"Om rommet i arkitekturen", Byggekunst 34, no. 6–7, 1952, pp. 97–101.

Park, Jin-Ho, "An Integral Approach to Design Strategies and Construction Systems—RM Schindler's 'Schindler Shelters'", Journal of Architectural Education 58, November 2004, pp. 29–38.

Postiglione, Gennaro, "Arne Korsmo: eget hjem. A traditional House", Arne Korsmo —Knut Knutsen. Due maestri del Nord, eds. Nicola Flora, Paolo Giardiello and Gennaro Postiglione, Rome: Officina edizioni, 1999, pp. 46–71.

Prytz, Jacob Tostrup, "Bolig– og hjeminnredning", Statens håndverk— og kunstindustriskole årsmelding 1952–1953, 1953–1954, Oslo: SHKS, 1955, (various pages) pp. 3–6.

Remlov, Arne, "48 m² leilighet", Bonytt, 1954, pp. 38–40.

Schindler, RM, "Reference Frames in Space", Architect and Engineer 165, no. 1, 1946, pp. 10, 40, 44–45.

"Schindler-Shelters", American Architect 146, May 1935, pp. 70–72.

Statens håndsverks og kunstindustriskole, årsmelding 1952–1953, 1953–1954, ed. SHKS, Oslo: SHKS, 1955.

Skjerven, Astrid, "'Material, Technique, and Requirements': Arne Korsmo's Flatware", Scandinavian journal of design history 6, 1996, pp. 54–61.

"Ny helhet", Arne Korsmo. Arkitektur og design, eds.

Jon Brænne, Eirik T Bøe and Astrid Skjerven, Oslo Universitetsforlaget, 2004, pp. 157–214.

Stang, Kaare, "Z for Zaitzow", 30 mins, Norway: Norsk Filminstitutt, 2007.

Statens håndverks og kunstindustriskole, årsmelding 1952-1953, 1953-1954, Oslo: SHKS, 1955.

Stenstadvold, Håkon, "Nederlag", Bonytt 9, 1949, pp. 54–55.

Teigen, Karl, "Nye sølvarbeider", bonytt 9, no. 5–6, 1949, pp. 81–85.

Tyng, Alexandra, Beginnings Louis I Kahn's Philosophy of Architecture, New York: Wiley, 1984.

Tømmervåg, Johan, "Hvem skapte byen?", Årbok for Nordmøre 2009, ed. Nordmøre historielag, Kristiandsund: Historielaget, 2009, pp. 17–30.

Utzon, Jørn, "Platforms and Plateaus: Ideas of a Danish Architect, Zodiac, 1962.

Weston, Richard, Utzon: Inspiration, Vision, Architecture, Hellerup: Edition Bløndal, 2002.

INDEX OF PROPER NAMES

ILLUSTRATIONS

Photographers:

Ane Hjort Guttu 8, 12, 14, 15 top, 17,18, 20–28, 29 bottom, 32- 35, 130, 137, 159, 162, 164, 180, 182
Espen Grønli 19
Finn Arne Johannessen 15, 16 bottom, 31, 122, 125, 127, 92, 144 left, 146 left, 147, 155, 158, 160, 161
Finn Fougner Kolstad 29 top, 134 top
Frode Larsen 11
Elisabeth Tostrup 10, 30, 65, 66 left, 121, 123, 126 bottom, 129, 132, 133, 135, 136, 143, 144 right, 146 right, 149 bottom

I would like to thank the following persons who made available privately owned photographs and drawings for reproduction:

Liv Eftesøl 86 top right
Lars Hurum 86 bottom
Grete Prytz Kittelsen and her heirs 37 bottom, 39, 43 bottom, 88 left, 152, 153
Terje Moe 64
Anna Maria Norberg-Schulz 57 left
Hanne Margrete Refsdal 52 right, 79 left, 83 right, 86 top left, 96–119, 141, 145, 151

I would also like to thank the following institutions who made available pictures for reproduction:

Bioforsk, the Norwegian Institute for Agricultural and Environmental Research (plant sciences division), signed Knut Quelprud, 139 left
National Museum for Art, Architecture and Design 37 top, 38, 40–43 top, 44–52 left, 53–55, 57 right, 59, 61 top, 69, 70–71, 74, 76–77, 80, 82, 87, 94, 120, 143
Oslo Agency for Planning and Building Services 124

Every effort has been made to trace all copyright holders but if any have been inadvertently overlooked please contact the publishers so that any necessary arrangements can be made at the first opportunity.

Alvar Aalto. Villa Mairea 1938–1939. 156 top right
Arne Korsmo. 1. ed. 6, 73 right, 81, 83 left, 89 bottom, 90, 93
Arne Korsmo. Arkitektur og design. 58, 60, 61 bottom, 70, 79 right, 91
A5 - meningsblad for unge arkitekter no. 9. 71 bottom left, 73 left
Blueprints for modern living: history and legacy of the case study houses. 66 right
Byggekunst 34, no. 12 (1952). 74 right

Byggekunst 37, no. 7 (1955). 150
Fallingwater: a Frank Lloyd Wright Country House.126 top
Grete Prytz Kittelsen: emalje – design. 85, 89 top
Japanska tehuset Zui-Ki-Tei, Etnografiske museet, Stockholm, 134 bottom
Journal of Architectural Education 58, November (2004). 149 top
Jørn Utzon: Arkitektens univers. 67.
Nordisk arkitektur. 156 top left and right
Scandinavian journal of design history 6 (1996). 88 right
Statens håndverks- og kunstindustriskole, årsmelding 1952–1953, 1953–1954. 75
Tempel und Teehaus in Japan. 138
Women and the Making of the Modern House. A Social and Architectural History. 63

COLOPHON

© 2014 Artifice books on architecture, the architect(s) and the author(s). All rights reserved.

First published in Norwegian in 2012 under the title *Planetveien 12. Arne Korsmo og Grete Prytz Kittelsens hus* by Pax Forlag, Postboks 461 Sentrum, 0105 Oslo, Norway.

Artifice books on architecture
10A Acton Street
London
WC1X 9NG

T. +44 (0)207 713 5097
F. +44 (0)207 713 8682
sales@artificebooksonline.com
www.artificebooksonline.com

All opinions expressed within this publication are those of the authors and not necessarily of the publisher.

Designed by Freddy Williams at Artifice books on architecture. British Library Cataloguing-in-Publication Data. A CIP record for this book is available from the British Library.

For Pax Forlag:
Editing: Live Cathrine Slang
Design: Anne Vines
Picture editing: Elisabeth Tostrup

This publication was supported by:
The Research Council of Norway
The Oslo School of Architecture and Design.

This translation has been published with the financial support of NORLA—Norwegian Literature Abroad, Fiction & Non-fiction.

ISBN 978 1 908967 48 0

No part of this publication may be reproduced, stored in a retrieval system, or transmitted, in any form or by any means, electronic, mechanical, photocopying, recording, or otherwise, without prior permission of the publisher. Every effort has been made to trace the copyright holders, but if any have been inadvertently overlooked the necessary arrangements will be made at the first opportunity.

Artifice books on architecture is an environmentally responsible company. *Planetveien 12, The Korsmo house. A Scandinavian* icon is printed on sustainably sourced paper.

Artifice
books on architecture